Water

SMITH & HAWKEN

The Hands·On *Gardener*

Water

by SUSAN MCCLURE
with illustrations
by JIM ANDERSON

WORKMAN PUBLISHING · NEW YORK

Library of Congress Cataloging-in-Publication Data
McClure, Susan, 1957–
Water / by Susan McClure.
p. cm.
ISBN 0-7611-1778-4 (alk. paper)
1. Landscape gardening--Water conservation--United States.
2. Drought-tolerant plants--United States.
3. Xeriscaping--United States.
I. Title
SB475.83 M33 2000
635.9'525—dc21   99-049810
CIP

Workman Publishing Company
708 Broadway, New York, NY 10003-9555
www.workman.com

Manufactured in the United States of America

First printing March 2000
10 9 8 7 6 5 4 3 2 1

Contents

WISE WAYS
to WATER

WATER-
CONSERVING
PLANTS

WATER *in* YOUR OWN BACKYARD

The gardener is never alone. Even if nobody else sets foot in the garden, the earth and the environment are constant companions. They change with the season, bringing new life and carrying away the old. The sun warms the shoulders on a crisp day and the rain mists the memory as it moistens the earth. The sun, wind, soil, songbirds, earthworms, and butterflies are as familiar as lifelong friends. They brighten most days with ready camaraderie but, as occasionally occurs in friendships, also may be headstrong and contrary. Nature's physical resources stand beside the gardener, providing the raw clay from which to mold a bed of flowers, or the processes by which those flowers need to grow.

Gardening makes a connection to the larger world around us— beyond deadlines and obligations. It opens the senses to the warmth and potent energy of the sun, the power of the rain, and the galloping passage of the seasons. It allows for combining the mind, body, soul, and spirit with the eternal elements of nature to communicate in the language of growth. One of the most powerful of these elements is water, which is essential for life in and out of the garden.

Water is transparent, tasteless, and odorless, yet powerful enough to carve the Grand Canyon from solid rock. A medium of contradictions, it runs with apparent freedom from the tap at home, but in the desert may only be found in the heart of a cactus. It may swamp the earth with drenching downpours one week only to leave it parched and languishing the next.

"Water, thou . . . canst not be defined, art relished while ever mysterious. Not necessary to life, but rather life itself, thou fillest us with a gratification that exceeds the delight of the senses," wrote French novelist Antoine de Saint-Exupéry. Where rainfall is abundant many of us take it for granted. While a brief, gentle April shower in Boston, Chicago, or Atlanta may produce the pleasures of which Saint-Exupéry writes, all too often spring rain arrives in seemingly endless torrents, making the garden too sodden for outdoor activities and bringing gray skies day after day.

But for the same blessing of rain, inhabitants of many drier parts of the country—including Tucson, Flagstaff, and Denver—would gladly put up with these minor irritations and more. While continual sun and blue skies may be perfect for picnics, they are also the escorts for drought. Without natural rainfall or a gardener's attention to watering, the soil dries up and the plants in it shrivel. Cracks open in sun-baked soil. Plants that were once plump and healthy are reduced to hollow, crumbling skeletons. The gardener must intervene, applying the gift of water with a conscientious hand.

The power to irrigate is one of the greatest forces in modern civilization. By defeating the effects of drought, it staves off famines and doubles the productivity of ordinary land. It allowed the rise of ancient Egyptian, Roman, and Aztec cultures as well as our own agricultural green revolution. Today, irrigated farmland produces about one-third of the world's food supply. Fully 90 percent of the apples, carrots, lettuce, and other fresh fruits and vegetables in the produce aisle at your grocery

THE WATER CYCLE

The flow of water is not confined to rivers or the inner workings of plants; it also circulates on a larger scale from the atmosphere to the earth and back. Approximately 300 million gallons of water change places constantly. Water evaporates from the ground—from lakes, rivers, even drippy faucets—and rises as water vapor into the atmosphere. It condenses into clouds—puffy white cumulus or dense dark thunderheads—and returns to earth in the guise of drizzle, rain, downpour, hail, sleet, and snow.

This moisture may soak down into the soil, percolating deep into underground aquifers. Or it may run off into drainage ditches, streams, rivers, and oceans. It may be absorbed into plants and transpire or evaporate back into the atmosphere.

For example, in Ohio, which averages 38 inches of rain per year, 10 inches run off into streams and rivers, 2 inches evaporate from the surface of the ground, and 26 inches soak down in the soil. Of the total water in the soil, 20 inches evaporate back into the atmosphere and 6 inches percolate down into subsurface groundwater supplies.

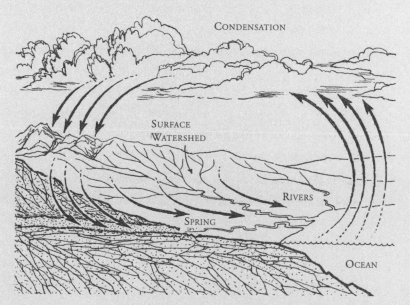

Water evaporates from the ground into the atmosphere, condenses into clouds, and falls back to earth as precipitation.

Source: *Ohio's Hydrologic Cycle* by Larry Brown; Ohio State University Extension Fact Sheet

store come from irrigated cropland. "There is . . . no doubt that irrigated agriculture is critical to our nation's and the world's food supply. Without productive irrigated agriculture, hundreds of millions of acres of rain forests and marginal lands in more humid areas would have to be cleared to produce food for the growing population," writes Thomas Trout of the USDA-Agricultural Research Service, in a recent *Journal of Soil and Water Conservation*.

If irrigating with a little water is good, then it stands to reason that using a lot would be better. Unfortunately, that is not the case. Water is a finite resource. More than 97 percent of the planet's water resides in the sea as salt water, and the remainder recycles from the atmosphere to the earth and back again. There will be enough water worldwide for good works only if we use ingenuity to increase the efficiency of irrigation.

WATER CONSERVATION

Conserving water is a critical task for the home gardener, and success depends largely on what is planted. Green lawns, succulent vegetables, thirsty perennials, newly planted trees and shrubs, and those greedy flowerpots that look so good on the patio all need water. When the rain that fell so relentlessly last weekend is only a memory, panting petunias and sulky impatiens will continue to demand water.

Instead of constantly reacting to a limp leaf or wilty bud by turning on the hose, a gardener can become proactive, planning ahead to avoid being a slave to the faucet. Shaving gallons off daily water use may be as easy as planting trees and shrubs that are naturally compatible with the local rainfall. Improving soils so they will retain moisture and mulching to slow the return of moisture to the skies can slow the drain on municipal

"If everyone in the Denver area would consciously work to conserve water, an estimated 83 million gallons could be saved every day. This would equal almost 13 billion gallons per year, enough to fill Mile High Stadium a mile high. That is a lot of water!"
—Denver Water Department Office of Water Conservation

water or well reserves and lower the water bill. Remember that mankind masters nature not by force but by understanding, according to British scientist Jacob Bronowski.

AVERAGE ANNUAL RAINFALL

STATE AND CITY	IN/YR	STATE AND CITY	IN/YR
Alabama, Birmingham	55	Nebraska, Omaha	30
Alaska, Anchorage	15	Nevada, Las Vegas	4
Arizona, Phoenix	7	New Hampshire, Concord	37
Arkansas, Little Rock	49	New Jersey, Atlantic City	40
California, San Diego	9	New Mexico, Albuquerque	8
California, San Francisco	19	New York, New York City	44
Colorado, Denver	15	North Carolina, Raleigh	42
Connecticut, Hartford	44	North Dakota, Bismarck	15
Delaware, Wilmington	41	Ohio, Cleveland	35
Florida, Jacksonville	53	Oklahoma, Oklahoma City	31
Georgia, Atlanta	49	Oregon, Portland	37
Hawaii, Honolulu	23	Pennsylvania, Philadelphia	41
Idaho, Boise	12	Rhode Island, Providence	45
Illinois, Chicago	33	South Carolina, Charleston	52
Indiana, Indianapolis	39	South Dakota, Rapid City	16
Iowa, Des Moines	31	Tennessee, Memphis	52
Kansas, Topeka	33	Texas, El Paso	8
Kentucky, Lexington	46	Texas, Houston	45
Louisiana, New Orleans	60	Utah, Salt Lake City	15
Maine, Portland	44	Vermont, Burlington	34
Maryland, Baltimore	42	Virginia, Richmond	44
Massachusetts, Boston	44	Washington, D. C.	39
Michigan, Detroit	31	Washington, Seattle	39
Minnesota, Duluth	30	West Virginia, Charleston	42
Mississippi, Jackson	53	Wisconsin, Milwaukee	31
Missouri, St. Louis	34	Wyoming, Casper	11
Montana, Billings	15		

Source: Tom York, Chief of Office of Surface Water, United States Department of the Interior

IDENTIFYING LOCAL WATER NEEDS: The first step in water conservation is to determine the average annual rainfall in your area and

VARIATIONS IN THE QUANTITY OF RAINFALL

SACRAMENTO, CALIFORNIA (DRIEST IN LATE SPRING AND SUMMER)

Winter:	January	4.03"	February	2.88"	March	2.06"
Spring:	April	1.31"	May	.33"	June	.11"
Summer:	July	.05"	August	.07"	September	.27"
Fall:	October	.86"	November	2.23"	December	2.90"

DENVER, COLORADO (DRIEST IN FALL AND WINTER)

Winter:	January	.51"	February	.69"	March	1.21"
Spring:	April	1.81"	May	2.47"	June	1.58"
Summer:	July	1.93"	August	1.53"	September	1.23"
Fall:	October	.98"	November	.83"	December	.55"

MOBILE, ALABAMA (DRIEST IN FALL)

Winter:	January	4.59"	February	6.48"	March	6.48"
Spring:	April	5.35"	May	5.46"	June	5.07"
Summer:	July	7.74"	August	6.75"	September	6.56"
Fall:	October	2.62"	November	3.67"	December	5.44"

BOISE, IDAHO (DRIEST IN SUMMER AND EARLY FALL)

Winter:	January	1.64"	February	1.07"	March	1.03"
Spring:	April	1.19"	May	1.21"	June	1.21"
Summer:	July	.95"	August	.40"	September	.58"
Fall:	October	.75"	November	1.29"	December	1.34"

CINCINNATI, OHIO (DRIEST IN LATE SUMMER AND FALL)

Winter:	January	3.13"	February	2.73"	March	3.95"
Spring:	April	3.58"	May	3.84"	June	4.09"
Summer:	July	4.28"	August	2.97"	September	2.91"
Fall:	October	2.54"	November	3.12"	December	3.00"

Source: Tom York, Chief of Office of Surface Water, United States Department of the Interior

Designed for arid soil, this drought-tolerant garden provides variety in form and texture.

find out whether it is prone to droughts. Examples of average annual rainfall for U.S. cities are listed on page 5. For more details, contact your local Cooperative Extension Service for the United States Department of Agriculture.

Variations in the quantity of rainfall occur season to season and month to month. Knowing the natural rhythm of rainfall in the region allows a gardener to plant when moisture is abundant.

XERISCAPING: When it comes to making the most of limited water, an arid-climate gardener has many resources. The challenges of creating a beautiful landscape despite precariously little water have spawned one of

Mapping your garden before you plant will help you make the most of available water.

PLANT KEY

1. *Dudleya brittonii*
2. *Sempervivum arachnoideum*
3. *Agave attenuata*
4. *Agave victoriae-reginae*
5. *Aeonium arboreum* 'Zwartkop'

the most exciting revolutions seen in horticulture—the birth of xeriscaping, or gardens designed to need little or no watering. Xeriscaping is not limited to dry lands, however. It focuses on selecting plants according to a region's rainfall.

In Denver, which receives only 13 to 15 inches of rain a year, water conservation has been a priority since the early 1980s. The Associated Landscape Contractors of Colorado and Denver Water joined forces to plan for future water limitations and began experimenting with ways to garden with minimal irrigation. Such gardening basics as mulching, building organic-rich soils, irrigating efficiently, and combining landscape plants according to their water needs quickly showed promise.

In 1983, Nancy Leavitt, an environmental planner for Denver Water, coined the word *xeriscape* to describe water conservation through creative landscaping. Like the name, the concept has spread throughout arid regions. Heavily irrigated Tucson gardens, lush 1970s landscapes of lawns and palm trees, now include drought-tolerant native species—a natural progression inspired, at least in part, by rising water bills. Today, Tucson has one of the lowest per capita rates of water use in the United States. The gardening techniques and drought-tolerant plants used in xeriscaping can encourage productive gardening anywhere.

WATER, THE FLUID *of* LIFE *for* PLANTS

Water, the pulse of the garden, slips unseen through every plant, running from soil to root to leaf and out. Just as a river catches a fallen branch in its flow, minute currents within plants pull in nutrients while eddies swirl sugars from leaves back to hungry roots. Water also kindles seed germination, photosynthesis, flowering, fruiting, and most other growth processes.

Juicy cucumbers and watermelon, which can quench your thirst on a hot summer day, are 90 percent water. Sweet, petite cherry tomatoes, which squirt sap and seeds with your first bite, are 95 percent water. So is lettuce, with its fast-growing, succulent leaves, the inner ones being the most moist and tender. Asparagus tips contain 88 percent water. Tender carrot roots, although not commonly considered juicy, can contain 88 percent water. Even the woody trunks of trees can be 50 percent water.

Water is composed of two hydrogen atoms, containing a single proton and an electron, fused tightly to an oxygen atom. This atomic trio makes charged molecules that, when in liquid form, cohere in a stream that can be pushed or pulled through a plant. Water easily passes from a liquid into a vapor, evaporating from leaves and, in its absence, pulling more water up from the roots. Cohesive water molecules also will sheathe clay, silt, and organic particles in the soil, creating reservoirs that can be tapped by plant roots. The electric charges in water make it a superior solvent to carry nutrients such as nitrogen within the soil and plant body.

NITROGEN AND WATER

Essential for plant growth, nitrogen is freely carried in water. As water cycles from rain to runoff, from evaporation and transpiration to percolation through the soil, so does nitrogen, which never stays quiescent. Because nitrogen in fertilizers can be washed out of the soil by heavy rain, there is potential for pollution, and reapplication for garden benefits is required.

Osmosis is a phenomenon in which water in the ground or plant body moves from areas that contain dilute aquatic solutions to areas concentrated with sugars, salts, or minerals. The power of this flow, called osmotic potential, pushes water from the earth into the plant's nutrient-filled root or seed and from the stem into the sugar-rich solution of a photosynthesizing leaf. Osmosis shuttles water between cells within a plant. As the moving force behind many diverse plant functions, it causes day-blooming water lilies to close at night and sunflowers to chase the brilliance of the sun across the sky.

Water is also fundamental to photosynthesis, the food-producing process that is the foundation for Earth's entire web of life. Light energy, which is captured by green chloroplasts in plants, powers the conversion of water and carbon dioxide into sugars that nourish plants and the animals that eat plants. Unlike the pollution emitted by factories, the by-product of this miraculous process is pure oxygen.

WATER'S ROLE IN PLANT LIFE

Water is a jack-of-all-trades that serves plants in many crucial capacities. Many of its roles are simple but ingenious.

HOW WATER POWERS TRANSPIRATION: Every pound of dry leaves—fallen autumn foliage of crimson and gold and herbal seasonings

WATER QUALITY

Free-flowing water is not pure H_2O, even if it comes from an artesian well. It contains, to a greater or lesser extent, souvenirs from where it has passed: water-soluble nutrients, sediment, and man-made leftovers such as fertilizers, pollutants, effluent from septic systems, and acids from airborne fossil fuel emissions.

Get to know the purity of local irrigation water from a well, municipal system, or nearby pond. This information will help you to make the most of existing water by heading off contamination problems, such as the following:

• Acidic water often picks up lead from older plumbing systems. It can also carry copper and zinc and make potting soil too acidic for good growth of most plants. When irrigating with acidic water, be certain to plant in potting soil that contains pH buffers or add a sprinkling of limestone to the soil to minimize acidity.

• Iron, which can give a pristine white bathtub a rust-colored black eye, most often comes from bedrocks such as iron pyrite and magnetite or rusty well casings. Although a nuisance in the house, iron-rich water generally causes no problems in the garden.

• Calcium, which is found in bedrocks such as feldspars and gypsum, is often accompanied by magnesium. These minerals clog pipes, create hard water, and change soil pH, sometimes making gardens too alkaline for good growth. Potting soil, which is most susceptible to problems from alkaline water, can be dosed with a sprinkling of sulfur to counteract the alkaline effect of calcium.

• Sodium, which is leached from feldspars and halite or released by sea water, can make the earth too salty for most plants. To minimize the damage sodium often causes, flush out the garden and potting soil well with water to wash away excess sodium.

preserved for winter—has consumed 300 to 500 pounds of water in its short lifetime. Even though most plants are gluttonous water consumers, they hold on to only 5 percent of the water they absorb. For instance, corn plants may lose more than one hundred times their own weight in water before the ears are ready to pick.

This apparent wastefulness is called transpiration, and it plays an important role in plant metabolism. Like a line of people inching along one step at a time in perfect synchrony, water moves into the root of a plant, up through the stem, and out by way of the leaf, in a process called mass flow. As moisture evaporates from the leaves, it pulls a cohesive stream of water up after it.

How much water is lost and subsequently replaced by mass flow depends primarily on the cells that guard the leaf pores, which are called stomata in botanical circles. Like guardians at a gate, these cells provide a fail-safe system. If the air gets hot and turbulent, which can dangerously increase evaporation, or the soil gets too dry and becomes unable to replace lost water, the guard cells will close the leaf pores. This allows the plant to preserve much of what water it presently contains.

Two kidney-shaped guard cells, each with one concave wall, fit together to make a stoma, or pore. Between them is an opening where evaporation occurs. When water is in short supply, they take on a rounder shape that shuts the opening. Closed stomata help spare the plant from wilting but do so at a cost. Carbon dioxide, which is needed for photosynthesis, cannot enter and food production drops dramatically.

Dry soil, hot air, low humidity, and high winds all can cause stomata to close. Summer heat, for instance, may wilt leaves on a squash vine, even one that has been watered recently. During a temporary wilt, the stomata should close; however, the stomata on older leaves may lose sensitivity and remain open, ignoring feedback and damaging the water-balancing system.

Certain plants of hot and arid regions, including stonecrops (*Sedum* spp.), life plant (*Kalanchoe* spp.), wax plant *(Hoya carnosa),* snake plant *(Sansevieria zeylanica),* Spanish moss *(Tillandsia* spp.), and bromeliads such as pineapples, open their stomata during the cool of the evening to minimize moisture loss. They gather up carbon dioxide, transform it into malic acid, and store it within water-filled organs called vacuoles until sunrise. When the sun is shining and the stomata are safely closed, the malic acid is converted into sugar.

Paul Kramer, author of *Water Relations of Plants,* views transpiration as an unavoidable evil. It powers the mass flow of moisture into the roots and up the stems of plants, but is capable of causing tremendous dam-

WATER pH AND PLANT PREFERENCES

Irrigation water can be either alkaline or acidic, and these conditions can change soil fertility, particularly when it is used on potted plants. The pH scale runs from 1 to 14, with 7 being neutral. Acidic water is rated from 1 to 6.9; alkaline water is 7.1 to 14. A soil with a pH of 6 is vastly different from one with a pH of 7; that single point represents an exponential increase in hydrogen ions and a jump from acidic to neutral. A jump to pH 8 brings soil into the alkaline range, where plants such as lavender and baby's breath prosper but rhododendrons and azaleas do not.

Home pH test kits can easily reveal the nature of irrigation water. More sophisticated water tests conducted at EPA-certified or state-certified laboratories can also identify total dissolved solids, iron, sulfur, and possible contaminants.

When you know your water and soil pH, you can grow plants with complementary pH preferences. Some examples are listed below.

pH PREFERENCES

American arborvitae	6 to 8
Colorado spruce	5 to 7
Crabapple	5 to 6.5
Dogwood	5 to 6.8
Douglas fir	6 to 7
English holly	4 to 5.5
Ginkgo	6 to 7
Honey locust	4 to 5.5
Red oak	4 to 6
Scotch pine	4 to 7
Star magnolia	5 to 6
Sugar maple	6 to 7.5
Sweet gum	6 to 7
Sycamore	6 to 7
Tulip tree	6 to 7.5
White oak	5 to 6.5
Witch hazel	6 to 7.5

Source: NMPro and Cyber conference workshop with Texas A&M, North Carolina State University, Oregon State University, and the Horticultural Research Institute of Ontario; Hanna Mathers, professor, Department of Horticulture at Oregon State University

age from dehydration. This damage, fortunately, can be prevented by careful garden water management.

WHERE'S THE WATER? An inner journey into plant cells reveals stockpiled water in aquatic oases such as the following:

• Fifty to 80 percent is stored in vacuoles, cavities filled with diluted cell sap. In fresh seeds like tender, juicy peas and beans, for instance, vac-

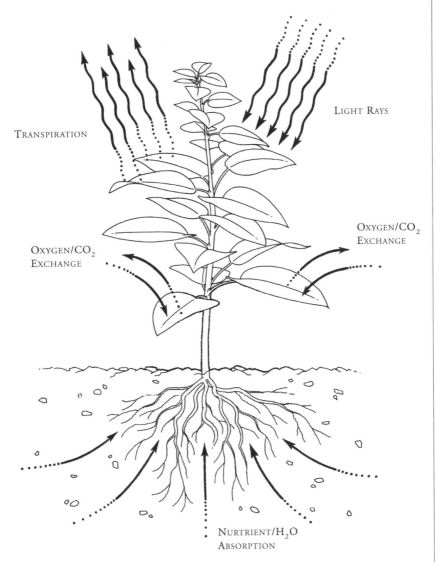

TRANSPIRATION

LIGHT RAYS

OXYGEN/CO$_2$
EXCHANGE

OXYGEN/CO$_2$
EXCHANGE

NUTRIENT/H$_2$O
ABSORPTION

In the presence of sunlight, water (taken up by the roots) and carbon dioxide (absorbed from the air by the leaves) are converted into food for the plant. Excess water and oxygen escape through leaf pores in the process of transpiration.

uoles may be large. As the seeds mature and dry, falling dormant for winter, the vacuoles shrink to next to nothing.

• Five to 40 percent is in the cell walls, the rigid outer coating that provides support to stems, leaves, and other plant parts. Thick-walled leathery leaves, such as those of the rhododendron (*Rhododendron* spp.), store the most moisture.

• Succulent plants may contain even more water. Desert-dwelling cacti, succulent euphorbias (*Euphorbia* spp.), and century plants (*Agave* spp.) fill entire thin-walled cells, which look a little like water balloons, with reservoirs of water.

• Ice plants (*Mesembryanthemum* spp.) hold water in icelike beads on the skin of the plant.

FOOD TRANSPORT: Like the small dumbwaiter once used to send dishes from the kitchen to upper floors of spacious homes, plants have shuttle systems for moving food around. Green leaves serve as a kitchen, producing sugars by photosynthesis. Their sweet concoctions cannot linger there, however, and must be pushed down into the working body of the plant. Transportation is provided courtesy of a process called pressure flow.

Using the power of osmosis (see page 10), water rushes into the areas where actively photosynthesizing leaves have stockpiled concentrated sugar solutions. In the process, the water overflows, pushing sap down and out of the leaves through interconnected tubelike cells into the rest of the plant. Pressure flow has been clocked moving as quickly as 20 to 40 inches per hour.

WATER'S ROLE IN GERMINATING SEEDS: "Just add water," a popular instruction for preparing convenience foods, appeals not just to busy human families but to some of Earth's other creatures as well. Among plants, this strategy is nothing new; seeds have been doing it for eons. Seeds are ingenious structures that can live for years in a state of dehydrated suspended animation—lingering deep in the soil or in a seed packet in a dry cupboard. When soaked by a spring rain in warming soil, they swell and take in up to twenty times their volume

TEMPERATURE FOR TEMPERAMENTAL SEEDS

"Many young gardeners and amateurs flounder befogged, attributing failure of crops in the garden, or want of health of plants in the green-house, to bad seeds, uncongenial soil or fertilizers, when it is much oftener the case that the cause is of a totally different nature, and entirely within their control," wrote horticulturist Peter Henderson in 1874 (*Practical Floriculture,* Orange Judd Company, New York). According to Henderson, the temperature must be right for the preferences of the seeds sown.

in water in preparation for growth.

The rate of water absorption is influenced by heat: the process often speeds up as the temperature rises. But plants are loath to follow rules, so there always are some variations.

Warmth-loving plants such as ageratum (*Ageratum Houstonianum*), begonias (*Begonia* × *semperflorens*), browallia (*Browallia speciosa*), vinca (*Catharanthus roseus*), spider flower (*Cleome Hasslerana*), and coleus (*Coleus Blumei* syn. *Solenostemon scutellarioides*) germinate best at temperatures of about 75° F. Lady's mantle (*Alchemilla mollis*) and astilbe (*Astilbe* × *Arendsii*), both of which are hardy perennials, germinate best when temperatures are 60 to 70° F. Lacy-leaved larkspurs (*Consolida ambigua*) are among the first to show themselves in spring, starting well at temperatures as low as 55° F.

When they take in water, seeds activate enzymes that dip into the pantry of stored food in the seed, pulling out choice tidbits for the embryonic plant. Nourished, the seedling begins to grow. After water fills the confines of the seed, it breaks free, usually cracking the seed coat with a swipe of the young root. Now oxygen pours in, allowing the seedling to grow even more quickly.

Changing from a self-sufficient seed to a seedling is a process ripe with peril, particularly if water is limited. Young roots and shoots are delicate tissues without much water-absorbing capacity, and they can shrivel and die if allowed to dry out for only a few hours. The soil must be kept moist, particularly near the surface. A few weeks later, when the roots have expanded and the plants have toughened in the sun and wind, seedlings become young plants that are better able to hold their own.

The attention given to watering nursery beds can turn a packet of seeds into a garden full of flowers—and more. American novelist Charles Dudley Warner wrote in 1871, "There is life in the ground; it goes into the seeds; and it also, when it is stirred up, goes into the man who stirs it."

WATERING SEEDS AND SEEDLINGS: A watering can full of warm, pure water can be a gardener's best ally when starting seeds. Once seeds are up and growing, it seems they can hardly get enough water, and to deny them this necessity is the fastest way to invite disaster. Here is a procedure for successfully sowing seeds and managing their water needs.

Supports raise the plastic covering, allowing seeds to sprout with plenty of growing room.

SOWING SEEDS INDOORS When you want to get a head start on the growing season, you can sow seeds of many annuals, perennials, vegetables, and herbs indoors. Seed sowing has become easier than ever before, thanks to the sterile, peat-based seed-starting mixes now available. They are light and airy, encouraging vigorous root growth and discouraging development of seedling rots and damping-off diseases that often attack in heavy and wet soils. These seed-starting mixes, however, need regular watering to prevent the seedlings from drying out.

A loosely tied plastic bag provides a hospitable environment for germinating seeds.

Before sowing seeds, premoisten seed-starting mixes, adding water generously until the peat is moist,

Label each cell before enclosing the container in plastic.

spongy, and able to cling in a ball when squeezed. If the mix, mistakenly oversaturated, becomes soggy and sodden, add more dry peat blend to dilute the moisture level. Use the moistened mix to fill flats, pots, cell packs, or other containers equipped with bottom drainage holes. Sow the seeds according to the directions on the packet label.

Maintaining moisture during the quiet period before the seeds germinate is easy when you cover the pot or flat with clear plastic wrap. Some seed-starting kits come with their own plastic top, which creates a greenhouselike environment that holds moisture inside. Once the seedlings are up and pushing against their water-conserving dome, it will have to be removed. At this point, the planting mix will dry out quickly. You should check the soil moistness often and water frequently; it is critical not to allow the peat to become parched.

You can water potted seedlings from above or below. Larger seedlings benefit from overhead watering. Gently drizzle the pot to soak the planting mix until extra moisture works its way through the soil and out the bottom drainage holes. A little runoff carries excess salts, cleaning the soil and encouraging healthy roots. To encourage thorough wetting, you can buy planting mixes that include wetting agents or add your own (see page 46).

Smaller seedlings, which might be disturbed by water from above,

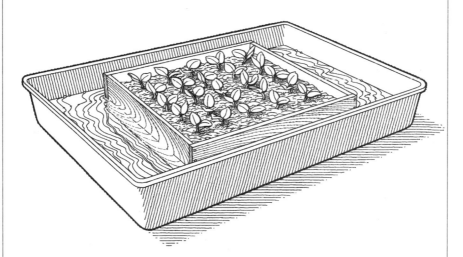

Bottom watering is best for smaller seedlings, but remove after 15 minutes and let excess water drain out.

can be watered from the bottom. Bottom watering is a sure cure for dry peat in a pot untended over a long weekend. Peat mix that has become shrunken and hard will resist rewetting and shed any water you pour over it. When you immerse the dry peat in water, however, the peat has no other alternative than to absorb it.

Cool fluorescent light fixtures can be hung using adjustable-length chains.

Place pots or packs containing seedlings in a saucer or flat filled with an inch or two of water, letting the potting mix soak up the water through the bottom drainage holes for 15 minutes or so. The job is not done, however, until you rescue the seedlings from the water and let the excess moisture drain out. Soil that is too wet can be as bad for seedlings as soil that is too dry.

Bright light is important for development of strong compact and bushy seedlings. In climates with plenty of sun, you can use a south-facing window as a seedling nursery. Where clouds often fill spring skies, a garden under a fluorescent shop light may be a better starting ground. Put the shop light just a couple of inches above the seedlings, setting it on an automatic timer to provide 14 to 16 hours of light each day. The more light seedlings receive, particularly warm sunlight, the more water they will use. Keep your watering can handy.

If you sow more than one seed per pot, transplant the young upstarts to individual pots before they become crowded. The ideal time is when they have two sets of true leaves. After loosening the roots in the soil, hold the base of the stem and gently tease the roots of neighboring seedlings apart. Fill new pots with premoistened planting mix and make a hole in the center to insert the seedling roots. Firm the seedling in place, positioning it so the stem and leaves emerge from the soil at the same level as when they first sprouted. You can moisten the soil lightly again to allow intimate contact between the roots and planting mix.

When the weather becomes warm enough for the seedlings to go

A TIMETABLE FOR SOWING SEEDS INDOORS

A schedule for sowing seeds is a secret to success and well worth noting on your calendar. That way, you won't forget when to start garden favorites such as coneflowers or cosmos. When sown right on time—neither too early nor too late—seedlings are mature enough to transplant easily but still young enough to grow vigorously when they make their garden debut.

COOL SEASON PLANTS

Start the following 8 to 10 or more weeks before planting out in moderate cool weather:

ANNUALS

Snapdragon *(Antirrhinum majus)*
Forget-me-not *(Myosotis sylvatica)*
Pansy *(Viola × Wittrockiana)*

VEGETABLES

Leeks *(Allium Ampeloprasum)*
Onions *(Allium Cepa)*
Scallions *(Allium Cepa)*

Start the following 6 to 8 weeks before planting out in moderate cool weather:

ANNUALS

China pinks *(Dianthus chinensis)*

VEGETABLES

Collards and kale *(Brassica oleracea)*

Start the following 4 to 6 weeks before planting out in moderate cool weather:

ANNUALS

Sweet alyssum *(Lobularia maritima)*
Stock *(Matthiola incana)*

VEGETABLES

Broccoli *(Brassica oleracea)*
Cabbage *(Brassica oleracea)*
Lettuce *(Lactuca sativa)*

WARM SEASON PLANTS

Start the following 8 to 10 or more weeks before planting out in frost-free weather:

PERENNIALS

Hollyhock *(Alcea rosea)*
Purple coneflower *(Echinacea purpurea)*

Daisy fleabane *(Erigeron spp.)*
Evening primrose *(Oenothera spp.)*
Golden coneflowers *(Rudbeckia spp.)*

ANNUALS

Wax begonia *(Begonia × semperflorens-cultorum)*

WARM SEASON PLANTS

Browallia *(Browallia speciosa)*

Vinca *(Catharanthus roseus)*

Lisianthus *(Eustoma grandiflorum)*

Heliotrope *(Heliotropium arborescens)*

Impatiens *(Impatiens Wallerana)*

Statice *(Limonium sinuatum)*

Bedding geranium *(Pelargonium × hortorum)*

Petunia *(Petunia × hybrida)*

VEGETABLES

Pepper *(Capsicum annum* var. *annuum)*

★ ★ ★

Start the following 6 to 8 weeks before planting out in frost-free weather:

PERENNIALS

'Summer Pastels' Yarrow *(Achillea × 'Summer Pastels')*

Lady's mantle *(Alchemilla mollis)*

Columbine *(Aquilegia* spp.)

Butterfly weed *(Asclepias tuberosa)*

Blackberry lily *(Belamcanda chinensis)*

English daisy *(Bellis perennis)*

'Early Sunrise' coreopsis *(Coreopsis* 'Early Sunrise')

Foxglove *(Digitalis* spp.)

Blanketflower *(Gaillardia × grandiflora)*

ANNUALS

Ageratum *(Ageratum Houstonianum)*

'Tropical Rose' canna *(Canna × generalis* 'Tropical Rose')

Spider flower *(Cleome Hasslerana)*

Globe amaranth *(Gomphrena globosa)*

Flowering tobacco *(Nicotiana* spp.)

Annual phlox *(Phlox Drummondii)*

Moss rose *(Portulaca grandiflora)*

Annual salvia *(Salvia* spp.)

Marigold *(Tagetes* spp.)

Mexican sunflower *(Tithonia rotundifolia)*

VEGETABLES

Eggplant *(Solanum Melongena)*

Tomato *(Lycopersicon Lycopersicum)*

★ ★ ★

Start the following 4 weeks before planting out in frost-free weather:

ANNUALS

Joseph's coat *(Amaranthus tricolor)*

Cockscomb *(Celosia* spp.)

Cosmos *(Cosmos* spp.)

Strawflower *(Helichrysum bracteatum)*

Nasturtium *(Tropaeolum majus)*

Zinnia *(Zinnia* spp.)

VEGETABLES

Cucumber *(Cucumis sativus)*

Melons *(Cucumis Melo)*

Pumpkin *(Cucurbita maxima)*

Squash *(Cucurbita* spp.)

Watermelon *(Citrullus lanatus)*

outdoors, transplants in spacious individual pots will be easy to pop out of their containers and into a snug hole in the garden. When you are transplanting them, fill the planting hole with water using a watering can or hose and settle the seedlings in. For the best results, water the transplants with a soaker hose or a hose with a fine spray attachment. The heavy droplets of a sprinkler may dislodge tiny seedlings from their new home; larger seedlings can be watered with a sprinkler that has a horizontal sprayer.

SOWING SEEDS OUTDOORS: Gardeners who always buy their seedlings prestarted miss out on the beauty of nature's grand plan. Seeds, dropped into a favorable soil and site, can spring to life when they are given enough heat and water. Many have no need for time-intensive indoor prestarting but like to take advantage of the low cost of growing seedlings—just a dollar or two for a seed packet yields dozens of seedlings.

As long as you prepare a fine-textured seed bed and attend to water-

PLANTS FOR DIRECT SOWING OUTDOORS

FLOWERS

Pot marigold (*Calendula officinalis*)
Larkspur (*Consolida ambigua*)
Spider flower (*Cleome Hasslerana*)
Cosmos (*Cosmos* spp.)
California poppies (*Eschscholzia californica*)
Blue fescue (*Festuca ovina*)
Dame's rocket (*Hesperis matronalis*)
Morning glory (*Ipomoea* spp.)
Sweet pea (*Lathyrus odoratus*)
Sweet alyssum (*Lobularia maritima*)
Flowering tobacco (*Nicotiana* spp.)
Love-in-a-mist (*Nigella damascena*)
Annual poppies (*Papaver* spp.)
Nasturtium (*Tropaeolum majus*)
Zinnia (*Zinnia* spp.)

VEGETABLES

Arugula (*Eruca vesicaria* subsp. *sativa*)
Beans (*Phaseolus* spp.)
Beets (*Beta vulgaris*)
Carrots (*Daucus Carota* var. *sativus*)
Corn (*Zea Mays*)
Cucumber (*Cucumis sativus*)
Lettuce (*Lactuca sativa*)
Melons (*Cucumis melo*)
Peas (*Pisum sativum*)
Pumpkin (*Cucurbita maxima*)
Radish (*Raphanus sativus*)
Spinach (*Spinacia oleracea*)
Squash (*Cucurbita* spp.)

ing, direct sowing of suitable seeds (see page 22) can be strikingly successful. When the weather is warm enough for the desired seeds and the soil has been well prepared—made fine and light with a rototiller and hoe—sow the seeds according to package directions.

If you plant during a rainy spell, nature may keep the soil moist while the seeds germinate and the seedlings become established. Should the weather turn dry, however, be prepared to water during this critical period. Overhead watering with a sprinkler, although easily accomplished, is not always the best option. The heavy droplets and runoff can wash away seeds and uproot small seedlings. Running a soaker hose beside the seedlings can be a gentler and more successful irrigation tactic. In a vegetable garden, as when sowing a new lawn, it can help to cover surrounding open soil with a layer of straw to minimize moisture losses.

How Plants Make the Most of Limited Water

About one-third of the world's land—including prairies, chaparrals, and deserts—is arid or prone to drought. Plants living in these areas must adapt or wither away, and those that prevail are ideal for water-conserving gardens. They make the most of limited water by expanding the reach of their roots or limiting water loss through adapted leaves.

Just as long arms and legs are an asset to a professional basketball player, deep or wide-spreading roots can expand the reach of plants in dry soils. The further roots penetrate, the more opportunity they have to tap into water reservoirs scattered through the soil. Prairie natives such as the cup plant (*Silphium perfoliatum*), for instance, spend most of their early years developing extensive roots; there is only a modest increase in shoot size until the roots are well underway. Tomatoes started from directly sown seeds may develop roots twice as deep as those of transplants from small pots—this advantage can keep them going during the dry days of summer.

Roots may develop alliances with terrestrial organisms such as fungal mycorrhizae to extend even further. Mycorrhizae, which spread in a threadlike network through some soils, pull in nutrients and other elements of the soil. Some rose nurseries sell mycorrhizae-inoculated roses that can transpire at higher rates than nonmycorrhizal plants.

Leaves adapt to drier conditions in a variety of ways. Fewer stomata on a leaf often lead to reduced moisture loss through transpiration. An oak (*Quercus* spp.), for example, is a particularly profuse user of water; it has about 100,000 stomata per square centimeter of lower leaf surface. In contrast, an apple tree may have only 30,000 stomata per square centimeter, and a corn leaf, with stomata on both the top and bottom, may have only 6,000 stomata per centimeter.

Small, fine, and needle-shaped leaves, which have less surface area from which water can evaporate, tend to minimize transpiration. Loblolly pines (*Pinus Taeda*) lose half the moisture of broader-leaved Northern red oaks (*Quercus rubra*). Silvery-hued leaves on plants such as lavender (*Lavandula* spp.) and lavender cotton (*Santolina Chamaecyparissus*) reflect sunlight to minimize heat and transpiration. Some hairy-leaved plants benefit from reduced wind flow, which helps reduce transpiration.

USING LEAF SHAPE TO ESTIMATE WATER NEEDS

The lavish taro leaf (*Colocasia esculenta*), which is 2 feet long and studded with millions of water-emitting stomata or pores, and other huge leaves are well suited for the swampy tropics but wouldn't last long in a desert. In regions where water is at a premium, leaves are reduced in size or, in the case of cacti, eliminated altogether to minimize water loss. The following pointers provide a general guide to the amount of water any given plant will need.

REQUIRES MORE WATER

Long leaves, particularly those over 12 inches long
Wide leaves, particularly those over 12 inches wide
Thin leaves
Leaves that wilt easily

REQUIRES LESS WATER

Succulent leaves
Leathery leaves
Silver leaves
Needle-shaped leaves
Minute leaves

MEASURING WATER IN THE GARDEN

The amount of water your garden will need varies with the region and season, kind of soil, and drinking habits of the plants within. Some general guidelines can help give you a better awareness of existing soil moisture so you can begin to determine what additional watering, if any, your garden will need.

RAINFALL QUANTITY

Measure the amount of rain that falls each week. Set a rain gauge, a clear cylinder marked with inches, in an open area of your yard or garden to gather its fill of nature's drizzles and drenchings. You can substitute straight-sided cans, such as coffee cans and tuna fish cans, as long as you measure their water content with a ruler.

Compare what nature has provided with a general idea of what garden plants will need. During the growing season, most gardens need at least an inch of rain a week, and more if the weather is hot, the soil is sandy, or the plants are young or densely planted. (For more on watering specifics, see chapters 5 and 6.)

DEPTH OF MOISTURE IN SOIL

Placement of water in the regions below ground will affect how much is available to plant roots. If rainfall is abundant, the soil will be deeply moistened naturally and able to nourish deep and shallow rooters alike. If rainfall is limited and irrigation is inadequate, the soil will not be thoroughly wet and plants can suffer as a result.

To determine how deeply the soil is moistened, dig down and measure the depth of the darker, damper part of recently moistened soil. Mature plants develop more self-sufficient roots if the soil is moistened to a depth of 8 inches or more. Young plants, which have not yet spread their roots, will need soil that remains moist near the surface.

Leaves are coated with a layer of wax called a cuticle. Some cuticles are thicker or more protective than others. As a general rule, a thicker cuticle reduces the amount of transpiration. According to a Texas A & M University study, low-maintenance roses (*Rosa hybrida*) such as 'Ferdy' and 'Pink Meidiland' had thicker cuticles and smaller leaves than 'Double Delight' and 'Paradise,' which allowed them to tolerate drought more readily.

WHEN WATER FALLS SHORT: Given the overwhelming presence of water in plants, it is easy to understand that sufficient water in the garden is more important than any spray, powder, or granule. Without water, plants simply will not grow.

When a plant becomes too dry, the leaves begin to droop and soft stems may actually swoon, flopping over the edges of the pot or falling flat on the ground. If watered immediately, the plant probably will recover. Even after it is standing up on its own, however, a once-wilted plant can show water-stress symptoms. Its roots may be damaged, reducing water uptake by 35 percent. If left wilted for any length of time, the entire plant will die no matter how much water is belatedly applied.

Even at an early stage before the plant wilts, water stress can make dramatic changes in plant performance. As stomata close, photosynthesis drops and nutrient uptake is curtailed, which weakens the plant. Without full vigor, it can become increasingly susceptible to attack by pests and diseases. Flowers and fruit may abort and new growth will stop.

It is to the gardener's advantage, therefore, to prevent damage from water stress through careful water management. Just how much water will be needed varies with the kind of plant and soil and is discussed in Chapter Three. More, in the case of water, is not always better.

DRAINAGE *and* SOILS

Always underfoot but seldom acknowledged, soil may seem something of a mystery. Soil is like the cluttered corner of a dark closet; the visual inaccessibility makes it easy to ignore. Unfortunately, this indifference limits future possibilities when it comes to gardening. In the growing of plants, the subterranean world is just as important as the air, sun, and other aboveground elements.

Brought to life in the rabbit warrens of Richard Adams's *Watership Down* and the underground explorations of Jules Verne's *Journey to the Center of the Earth,* the soil-bound netherworld resembles a distorted mirror image of the universe. It harbors elements such as air, water, and wildlife but in a fashion entirely different from aboveground. The atmosphere below, for indeed there is one, is created by oxygen, carbon dioxide, and other gases that filter through the pores between soil particles. They share this space with water, which sheaths soil particles and nourishes plant roots.

Many of us begin to explore this domain as children. Curious about spaces they cannot see—attics full of boxes, shadows beneath the bed—

children set out into the backyard with a shovel in hand. Holes dug yield a harvest of earthworms, grubs, and other subterranean creatures, treasures for keeping in jars and observing under a magnifying glass. Excavations reveal the long, fleshy, white taproot of the dandelion, which is able to burrow deep into moist soil depths and regenerate from small pieces left behind after weeding. They unearth the wiry, shallow thickets of grass roots, which rely on surface moisture for their sustenance.

Merely digging in the earth provides lessons in soil science. A hole gouged out of dense clay may fill up with the first rain; gardeners call this bathtub effect poor drainage. Afternoon play in a sandbox teaches about the largest of soil particles. Within hours of a drenching rain, sand may again become loose and warm, demonstrating a gardening principle called sharp drainage.

In *My Summer in a Garden* (1871), Charles Dudley Warner envisions the making of mudpies as one of mankind's best instincts. His ageless insight has proven its truth in garden after garden over the last century. Fortunately, adulthood does not always quench the thirst for the earthly explorations that have so much benefit for the garden. This chapter digs into the power of the earth and its capacity to harbor water.

UNDERGROUND
WATER FLOW

Something is happening beneath our feet, even now, unsensed but vital to the workings of the garden. It is water moving in tiny trickles that sift through miles of microscopic soil pores.

Gravity powers some water flow, pulling it downward after a drenching rain. Water oozes through large pores between soil particles and soaks deep into loose earth. Layers of rock or hard clay, like the sidewalk curb beside the road, can limit this downward movement. Impermeable barriers are particularly common in dry climates, where the lack of soil moisture creates an underground cementlike layer called hardpan, or caliche.

In addition to dancing to the pull of gravity, water moves through the soil energized by capillary action. Water molecules cling tightly into

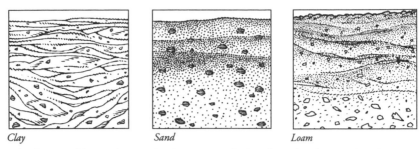

Clay   Sand   Loam

The density of fine rock particles determines whether the soil is clay, sand, or loam.

cohesive streams; this is the same phenomenon that drives transpiration within plants (see page 11). Regardless of the effect of gravity, sheets of water coat soil particles and provide most of the moisture available to thirsty plant roots.

Capillary action works most effectively in the pores between small and medium-sized soil particles such as clay and silt. In tight clay soils, however, capillary water may be abundant but the pores are too small for the roots to penetrate; therefore, the water goes unused. Resisting gravity's effects, poorly drained clay soils fill up with excess water, become oversaturated, and smother plant roots.

The large pores, plentiful in sandy soils, have little capillary action. Water drains out quickly at the beck and call of gravity. These soils are likely to become parched when rain or irrigation is infrequent, creating a difficult situation for many plants.

In a good soil—the well-drained and moist blend experienced gardeners know will yield outstanding performance—half of the porous space is filled with capillary water, and the other half is filled with air—two elements vital for plant life. Gravitational and capillary actions combine to produce prime conditions for rooting, and a strong root system produces the foundation needed for outstanding plant growth.

SCULPTING THE EARTH: Water has the power to move towering mountains, carve deep valleys, and make ever-changing patterns on flood plains. Driven by gravity, rain and melted snow wash down from hills and mountaintops, pulling along soil, gravel, and other elements of earth and etching the land. Rivers work in a similar way, catching sediment from riverbeds and pulling it downstream toward the sea.

According to journalist Charles Kuralt, the Mississippi River transports soil over 2,000 miles from thirty states to the Mississippi Delta, where it drops 500 million tons annually. "The business of the Mississippi, which it will accomplish in time, is methodically to transport all of Illinois to the Gulf of Mexico," he wrote in *A Life on the Road*.

Water can also leach out soluble minerals from solid rock to create caves and caverns like those that inspired Mark Twain's adventures with Indian Joe or thrill visitors to New Mexico's Carlsbad Caverns and Kentucky's Mammoth Cave. Underground springs and rivers saturate bedrock and fill weak crevices in water-soluble limestone and other stones, then slowly carry the minerals away. The results are just another example of water's artistic powers.

THE SOIL CONNECTION, A POWERFUL VARIABLE

Every garden begins with the mystery of what kind of soil lurks below the ground. Knowing the character of the soil, its virtues and flaws, is the first vital step toward managing its moisture levels. Is it loose, airy, and dry, or thick and moist?

With experience, a gardener can feel the soil and get clues about its content. But at best, a hands-on textural test is a general guide, like peeking at the surface of a cake to see if it is done. For an in-depth analysis, a professional soil test is required.

Basic soil tests that use dry soil samples mailed to specialty laboratories usually provide information on soil acidity and levels of phosphorus and potassium. For an extra fee, which is well worth the cost, an analysis of other nutrients and soil texture can be performed to determine percentages of sand, silt, and clay. To find a soil lab, contact the nearest Cooperative Extension Service office, which is usually listed under federal or county government in the Yellow or Blue Pages. Some labs are listed on the Internet and are easy to find by searching for keywords such as soil+test.

CLUES TO SOIL MOISTURE

Farmers and horticulturists often use soil moisture probes to identify moisture levels and determine when irrigation is necessary. At home, gardeners can use a less exact but still informative estimating system based on soil feel and appearance.

SOIL TYPE	CONDITION	CHARACTERISTICS
Sand and Sandy Loam	Dry	Loose, dry, flowing
	Wilting point*	Crumbs break into grains; will not compact into a ball
	50 percent	Can squeeze into a ball but won't stay
	100 percent, or field capacity	Squeezing leaves wet outline on hand; ball crumbles when pressed
Loam and Silt Loam	Dry	Powdery
	Wilting point	Crumbly, compresses into a ball
	50 percent	Compresses into a ball, can be slick
	100 percent	Squeezing leaves wet outline on hand; compressed ball is pliable and slick
Silty Clay Loam and Clay Loam	Dry	Hard and cracked
	Wilting point	Compressed ball holds together but is slightly crumbly
	50 percent	Compressed ball can be squeezed into a ribbon between thumb and forefinger
	100 percent	Squeezing leaves wet outline on hand; compressed ball easily makes ribbons

*See "Quantifying Soil Moisture in the Garden," on page 37, for definitions of wilting point and field capacity.

Source: University of Nebraska, Lincoln, Cooperative Extension Service's *NebGuide*, "Estimating Soil Moisture by Appearance and Feel," by Norman Klocke.

Deciphering what has been learned from the soil test is the next step. Among other factors, soil texture and structure affect how much water the soil can hold, how quickly water drains away, and how easily plant roots can tap into it.

 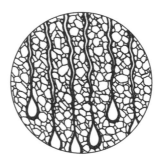

Soil containing compost (left) tends to hold water better than ordinary soil (right).

SOIL TEXTURE: Using hard-and-fast numbers, soil texture is defined objectively by the percentage of three different sizes of mineral particles that are found in the soil. It includes large particles of sand, which encourage quick water drainage, medium-sized particles of silt, and fine particles of clay, which can hold capillary water. A moist and well-drained loam soil, which mixes all three and capitalizes on their best qualities, could include 40 percent clay, 30 percent silt, and 30 percent sand.

Heavier-textured soils are more generous in their clay content, accommodating more than 40 percent clay particles and less than 45 percent sand or silt particles. Fine particles hold moisture, which is a benefit during dry weather, but they also may drain poorly, causing problems during wet weather.

Sandy soils have less than 15 percent clay or silt. Loose and light, they quickly shed excess moisture; however, they hold precious few reserves for dry spells.

SOIL STRUCTURE: Like furniture in a house, soil particles can be arranged in an infinite variety of ways, the organization of which is called soil structure. The best soils occasionally occur naturally but more frequently are created with generous additions of compost and feel loose and spongy. Sheer mineral soils, such as red Georgia clay and desert sands traversed by Arabian stallions, lack this magical quality.

The key to good soil structure is humus, organic matter left by decaying plant and animal life. As little as 5 percent organic matter can alter soil characteristics for the better. It changes isolated mineral particles into crumbs, which are not crumbly at all. Smaller clay and silt particles cluster around a central core of organic matter. They form relatively large aggregates that are separated by spacious pores. Water, air, and plant roots can move more freely. Therefore, humus makes heavy clay soils become lighter and sandy soils hold more water in the form of capillary reserves.

Soil crumbs are not held together permanently. Abusing the soil by watering with salty irrigation, tilling when it is too wet, or leaving it barren beneath pounding rain can shatter crumbs into smaller pieces.

PROBLEM SOILS FROM ARID CLIMATES: Among the most difficult soils for gardening are those found in arid climates. The combination of poor drainage and lack of soaking rains can cause the buildup of salts that damage plants and soil alike. This problem can be minimized by xeriscaping—growing drought-tolerant plants that need little irrigation and are less likely to aggravate soil problems.

AN EASY DRAINAGE TEST

To identify how quickly the soil drains, try this easy and revealing percolation test. Let the soil dry out, covering it with plastic for several days if necessary.

Dig a hole 1 foot deep and 2 feet wide and fill it with water. Watch how long it takes for the water to evacuate.

- 1 to 30 minutes: well-drained
- 30 minutes to 4 hours: moderate drainage
- Over 4 hours: poorly drained

Irrigation water, which holds dissolved salts, evaporates from the soil surface and leaves behind the salts. In the southwestern United States, irrigation water is salty enough to contribute as much as 10 tons of salt to each irrigated acre each year. Without soaking rain to wash away the salts, they accumulate and reach unhealthy levels. They burn plant roots and make soil water less available; as a result, plant growth steadily diminishes as salt levels increase.

SOME SALT-TOLERANT PLANTS

In saline soils of arid climates, seaside gardens, or salty berms beside cold-climate roads, some of the following plants may grow:

Date palm (*Phoenix dactylifera*)
Beet (*Beta vulgaris*)
Kale (*Brassica oleracea acephala*)
Asparagus (*Asparagus officinalis*)
Spinach (*Spinacea oleracea*)
Rugosa rose (*Rosa rugosa*)
Saltbush (*Atriplex* spp.)
Hackberry (*Celtis* spp.)
Green ash (*Fraxinus pennsylvanica*)
Kentucky coffee tree (*Gymnocladus dioica*)
Sea thrift (*Armeria* spp.)
Blue grama grass (*Bouteloua gracilis*)
Tall fescue (*Festuca arundinacea*)

SOIL PROFILE: THE CHANGING NATURE OF TERRESTRIAL DEPTHS: Like a seven-layer cake, mature soil is not a uniform entity but a sequence of strata that range from topsoil to pure rock. The top layer, bridging the gap between the geological region below and the world of life above, is topsoil, a blend of mineral and organic matter. Heavily modified by the living world, topsoil accommodates and anchors plant roots. Lower layers, primarily different types of stone, are the parent material for the soil and provide it with different chemical and physical characteristics.

The surface layer, called the "O" horizon, consists primarily of organic material. It is easy to observe in a deciduous woodland, where the loose leaves that litter the soil surface break down into dark, moist humus several inches below.

Organic matter mixes with mineral particles in the next layer, the "A" horizon. The upper portions of this layer, which tend to be loose and dry, teem with plant roots and subterranean life. At the bottom of the "A" horizon, fine clays and small particles collect and have a thicker and moister composition that can be less desirable for rooting.

The subsoil, or "B" horizon, is a dense conglomerate of water-deposited clay and other fine particles. Where soils are heavy, poorly drained, or compacted, it can develop into a hardpan or caliche that water cannot penetrate.

Weathered bedrock, or the "C" horizon, holds little potential for plant growth and lies just above bedrock, which is solid stone.

SOIL MOISTURE LEVELS

The amount of moisture in the soil, which like a rain-swollen river rises and falls according to the weather, influences what plants will grow, how quickly they will grow, and how well they will perform. Extreme soils, which are so saturated that they will suck a boot right off your foot or so deathly dry that they are ribboned with yawning cracks, are tolerated by limited numbers of plants and for limited amounts of time.

Soils with moderate levels of moisture, which can vary from light to lush, usually are the best for gardening. They may change as the soil grows drier after rainfall, or be fairly consistent, reflecting the soil's character. A sandy soil, for instance, tends to stay on the lean side, and a clay soil tends to be moist and rich like a devil's food cake.

It's common for horticulturists to recommend gardening in evenly moist soil. Paul Kramer, in the classic text *Water Relations of Plants,* states that major fluctuations in moisture are a conspicuous deficiency in the growth of potted greenhouse research plants. The same is true of most other potted plants, excepting cacti and succulents, which may tolerate dry soils for weeks.

But it is much less common for horticulturists to define the often-recommended term "evenly moist soil." While it is almost impossible to keep soil moisture truly and unchangeably even in the strictest sense, an evenly moist soil is one that never dries out or becomes saturated.

How much water it takes to maintain a middle ground depends on factors such as soil type, temperature, size of plant, and rate of growth. Rich soils with abundant compost are able to hold extra moisture reserves and are perfect for pots of forced spring flowering bulbs that thrive in damp but well-drained soils. In contrast, an airier potting mix high in sphagnum peat and vermiculite is ideal for rex begonias (*Begonia* Rex-Cultorum Hybrids) and scented geraniums (*Pelargonium* spp.), whose roots need to dry out slightly before being watered again. Larger potted plants, especially those growing quickly or transpiring heavily, will need to be watered more often to maintain an evenly moist soil. Root systems with limited soil space—foliage packed into small pots or intensively planted gardens—also will need more frequent watering.

Watering whenever it comes to mind is generally not sufficient to maintain even moisture. Some effort must be made to monitor natural rainfall and how much water plants are using. A rain gauge, a cylinder that catches and measures rainfall, can keep track of Mother Nature's contributions to the cause.

Feeling the dampness of the soil (see page 31) and watching for signs of slowing growth due to water shortages can give the gardener a sense of when water is needed. Early signs of impending water stress include lowering leaf angles, slight curling of the leaf blades, slowing growth, and changes in leaf color. Waiting until a plant wilts, although an undeniable clue that water is needed, is too late when the goal is maintaining evenly moist soil.

In a hypothetical typical garden, an inch of water each week is recommended to sustain a healthy landscape. Because few gardens will have the same water needs as a hypothetical typical one, water input must be adjusted for each site. Sandy soils and quick-growing warm-season plantings will likely need more water, while heavy soils in cool weather will need less (also see page 32).

The effort it takes to maintain even moisture may not be needed in every case. An easy-care garden may use plants such as hackberries (*Celtis occidentalis*) and daylilies (*Hemerocallis* spp.) that are well adapted to naturally fluctuating levels of rainfall, instead of relying on carefully applied water. A high-performance garden, however, in which the best potatoes, cucumbers, and petunias stand up and salute with exceptional vigor, is likely to need evenly moist soil and irrigation.

A gardener should be able to choose between growing plants that need even moisture and those that can do without. The former will require a larger investment of time and water, and each gardener must determine for him- or herself whether it is worthwhile.

QUANTIFYING SOIL MOISTURE IN THE GARDEN: Farmers and nurserymen work hard to keep moisture at ideal levels. They realize that control of soil moisture is an effective way to maximize plant performance and profits, and prefer to use analytic measurements of soil moisture instead of guesswork to know when to water.

Although a garden is more than the sum of its parts, mathematics hints at the complexity of the soil-water-plant relationship and helps interpret it. Combined with transpiration data for the crop grown, which varies with crop maturity and weather, and soil water-storage potential, growers and soil scientists can calculate when irrigation is necessary to maintain optimum growth.

Some of their analytical terms explain what is happening to soil moisture reserves and can help home gardeners understand these important dynamics.

Field Capacity: Several days after a drenching rain, when excess water drains away, soil reaches its field moisture capacity: water occupies 40 to 60 percent of the open soil pores and remains fairly consistent, providing optimum conditions for plant growth. In a sandy soil, field capacity is reached when soil moisture averages 9 percent; in a sandy loam, 14 percent; in a loam, 22 percent; in a clay loam, 27 percent; and in a clay, 35 percent.

Permanent Wilting Percentage: This is the point at which soil moisture levels drop so far that plants wilt. It is to be avoided if plants are to achieve their maximum potential. In a sandy soil, permanent wilting occurs when water levels fall to about 4 percent; in a sandy loam, 6 percent; in a loam, 10 percent; in a clay loam, 13 percent; and in a clay, 17 percent.

Readily Available Water: The field capacity minus the permanent wilting percentage reveals the amount of water available for plant use and evaporation. Heavier soils tend to store a wide range of readily available water, while sandy soils, with lower field capacities, have less readily available water. The amount of stored water can be increased, however, by growing deep-rooting plants or modifying the soil to hold more moisture (see page 42).

DRY OR KILLING DRY?

"The old gardener with whom my first essay in gardening was made used to define the difference in dryness in plants as 'dry' and 'killing dry'; 'dry' was the proper condition that the plant should be in, when water was applied, the surface indicating dryness by becoming lighter, but no flagging or wilting; but woe betide the unfortunate that allowed a plant to change to become in the condition of 'killing dry'; this in his eye was an unpardonable offense."

Peter Henderson (*Practical Floriculture*, 1874)

MAKING THE MOST OF THE SOIL

Gardeners may want to adopt the Boy Scout motto "Be Prepared," since every region will experience its own growth-slowing droughts or soil-flooding monsoons. Having soil that not only drains well but also retains moisture allows the garden to thrive during weeks of gray drizzle as well as parching sunshine.

IMPROVING SOIL DRAINAGE: There are many lessons to be learned during the times of spring rains. Just after the snow has melted or after a week of heavy rains, additional April showers can fill soils to the brim with moisture. Poorly drained soil that lacks the capacity to move excess water along will become swampy. Puddles may form in low places, below raised beds, or beneath gutters, saturating the soil with water and eliminating essential air. Some plants may tolerate occasional swampings, but others will die during this precarious season.

It isn't necessary to rely on luck or nature when a garden is planned in poorly drained soil. Adding extra organic matter to tight soils such as clay can improve the soil structure by encouraging small particles to clump into larger aggregates. Working in a 3- or 4-inch-deep layer of compost and sand, which is sold by some topsoil dealers in preblended mixes, is an easy way to make sweeping changes in the texture and structure of clay soils.

In regions where impermeable subsoil layers limit water movement, dig deep to break them up. The classic cure is double digging, which works the soil to a depth of 2 feet, and requires both a strong back and a drive to exercise.

Mark off the area you plan to dig, and water the soil well. A few days later, remove weeds and loosen the top inch or so. The next day, begin digging by creating a trench 1 foot wide and 1 foot deep. Remove the topsoil, loosen the exposed subsoil, and cover it with a shovelful of organic matter. Transfer the topsoil from the next trench you dig onto the subsoil of the first trench, and continue working the length of your marked-off area. Some gardeners spread compost over the entire bed when they're done. Continue in this way until you come to the end of your garden, where you will fill in the topsoil in the final topsoil strip with earth from the wheelbarrow.

Double digging loosens the soil to a depth of 2 feet below the surface. This method corrects poor drainage and creates a fertile planting area that's well worth the effort.

A garden fork can also be used to break up hard undersoil layers. Stab it into the ground and rock back and forth. Planting deep-rooted plants such as alfalfa may do the job without any stress or strain on the gardener.

To minimize problems with overabundant rainfall, a dry well (a hole 3- to 4-feet deep filled with gravel) can divert water to leave surrounding areas safely drained.

Perforated subsurface drainage pipes that run beneath the entire yard or are set beneath an area with problem drainage can take excess water to a storm sewer or drainage ditch. Although expensive to install, these pipes provide a nearly permanent solution to poor drainage; however, they will carry away rainwater in dry as well as wet seasons and may contribute to increased irrigation needs during drought.

A gentle swale or trench carved in a slight slope can carry excess surface water to a roadside ditch or retaining basin. If landscaped with bank-holding ornamental grasses or red-stemmed willows (*Salix alba* var. *vitellina* 'Britzensis'), a drainage ditch can be an attractive part of a naturalistic landscape.

Elevating a garden bed even a few inches above the surroundings will allow excess water to drain off, keeping the uplifted soil crown airy and dry. Raking vegetable garden soil into raised wide rows allows high productivity even during swampy spring weather. Beds raised even higher and held in place by retaining walls of timbers, brick, or stone may become so dry they need extra irrigation when rainfall is limited.

A final option is to plant species that will tolerate occasional swamping. Some examples come from Cornell Plantations in New York. These species withstood ten days of flooding in 4 to 10 inches of water and may work well for other occasionally soggy wet areas:

Red maple (*Acer rubrum*)

Cornelian cherry dogwood (*Cornus mas*)

White ash (*Fraxinus americana*)

Thornless honey locust (*Gleditsia triacanthos* var. *inermis*)

Black walnut (*Juglans nigra*)

Dolgo crabapple (*Malus* 'Dolgo')

White mulberry (*Morus alba*)

American sycamore (*Platanus occidentalis*)

Cottonwood (*Populus deltoides*)

White willow (*Salix alba*)

Pussy willow (*Salix discolor*)

European littleleaf linden (*Tilia cordata*)

Red cedar (*Juniperus virginiana*)

Pfitzer juniper (*Juniperus chinensis* var. 'Pfitzerana')

Japanese barberry (*Berberis thunbergii*)

Gray-stem dogwood (*Cornus racemosa* syn. *C. paniculata*)

Regel privet (*Ligustrum obtusifolium* var. *regelianum*)

Arrowwood (*Viburnum dentatum*)

Sweet viburnum (*Viburnum lentago*)

American cranberry bush (*Viburnum trilobum*)

Source: R. M. White, "Plant Tolerance in Standing Water: an Assessment," *Cornell Plantations* 28:50–52, 1973

MICROCLIMATES: VARYING SOIL CONDITIONS WITHIN THE GARDEN:

The soil can vary from one side of your yard to the other or even within a single garden, and as its texture and structure change so does the availability of moisture and nutrients. Even minor differences can influence garden success.

Elevated or mounded parts of the garden will have better surface drainage, minimizing the risk of oversaturated soils in wet weather, whereas sunken or slightly dished areas of the garden will collect moisture and stay wetter than elevated surroundings, which is a benefit during dry weather.

Slopes, especially those with topsoil eroded away, will be drier than flat areas and are ideal for planting with drought-tolerant plants. Open

TREES AND PLANTS PREFERRING WET OR DRY SOILS

Just as some people prefer warm or cold weather, certain plants grow better in dry or moist soils. Matching plant preferences to soil moistness is an important part of planning an easy-care landscape.

TREES AND SHRUBS FOR MOIST SOILS

Note: Most of these species prefer well-drained moist soils. Only a few, such as willows, sycamores, and river birches, will tolerate wetter soils.

Red maple (*Acer rubrum)*
Sugar maple (*Acer saccharum)*
Red chokeberry (*Aronia arbutifolia*)
River birch (*Betula nigra*)
Carolina allspice (*Calycanthus floridus*)
Sweet pepperbush (*Clethra alnifolia*)
Gray-stem dogwood (*Cornus racemosa*)
Red osier dogwood (*Cornus stolonifera*)
Honey locust (*Gleditsia triacanthos* var. *inermis*)
Kentucky coffee tree (*Gymnocladus dioica*)
Witch hazel (*Hamamelis* spp.)
Winterberry (*Ilex verticillata*)
Virginia sweetspire (*Itea virginica*)
Spicebush (*Lindera Benzoin*)
Sweet gum (*Liquidambar Styraciflua*)
Northern bayberry (*Myrica pennsylvanica*)
Sour gum (*Nyssa sylvatica*)
Sycamore (*Platanus occidentalis*)
Poplars (*Populus* spp.)
Swamp white oak (*Quercus bicolor*)
Pin oak (*Quercus palustris*)
Willows (*Salix* spp.)
Bald cypress (*Taxodium distichum*)
Viburnums (*Viburnum* spp.)

TREES AND SHRUBS FOR DRY SOILS

Note: For more information on selecting plants for dry soil, see page 104.

Amur maple (*Acer Ginnala* syn. *A. tataricum* subsp. *Ginnala*)
Lead plant (*Amorpha canescens*)
Japanese barberry (*Berberis thunbergii*)
Northern catalpa (*Catalpa speciosa*)
Hackberry (*Celtis occidentalis*)
Russian olive (*Elaeagnus angustifolia*)
Green ash (*Fraxinus pennsylvanica*)
Sea buckthorn (*Hippophae rhamnoides*)
Aaron's beard-Saint-John's-wort (*Hypericum calycinum*)
Rocky Mountain juniper (*Juniperus scopulorum*)
Japanese black pine (*Pinus thunbergiana*)
Swamp white oak (*Quercus bicolor*)
Bur oak (*Quercus macrocarpa*)
Staghorn sumac (*Rhus typhina*)
New Mexico locust (*Robinia neomexicana*)

areas used for mounding up extra clippings, autumn leaves, and weeds will be rich and moist from the organic matter and are ideal for growing moisture- and nutrient-hungry crops.

Buildings can influence the microclimate as well. For example, construction sites where the topsoil has been removed may harbor dense and poorly drained subsurface clay. Only a limited selection of plants can tolerate this footing unless amended.

Around the perimeter of a structure, where sand has been used as fill, the soil will stay drier. The site can become especially drought-prone if a roof overhang blocks direct rainfall.

And if leaves and debris clog a rain gutter, rain will run over the edge and down on the soil below, keeping it moister, even waterlogged. Good drainage and occasional gutter cleaning will help make this a successful garden site.

INCREASING MOISTURE RETENTION: While water retention is not necessarily a good thing in terms of human health, in gardening it can make an ordinary soil rich. No secret formula or high-tech product is needed for this transformation, just the addition of organic matter. Good choices include compost or well-rotted vegetables and deciduous leaves. These products of natural decay can double the water-holding capacity of the soil.

Work a layer of compost several inches deep into the top 8 inches of soil before planting. Because compost is continually decaying into nutrient soup, at least another inch of organic matter will be needed each consecutive year—more in warm climates and for stiff or dry soils. Organic matter can be worked into annual beds or layered like mulch on existing perennial, shrub, and tree beds.

Taking the short cut of merely working a few scoops of compost into individual planting holes can actually prove a disservice in the long run. It may keep the immediate planting area moister but, in doing so, can discourage plants from rooting out into the soil beyond. Limited root systems are the first to suffer in times of drought.

Gardeners without the time or facilities to make their own compost can purchase it. Many communities recycle municipal leaves and will sell and deliver the resulting compost by the cubic yard. Another great source of ready-to-use organic matter is the spent compost from mushroom farms, which is popular in Chicago, Philadelphia, and other areas where mushrooms are grown commercially.

For smaller jobs, you can buy bags of peat moss, composted cow manure, and leaf compost at garden centers and do-it-yourself home centers. Discount stores often have spring and fall sales on bagged organic matter, so those seasons are great times to stock up.

Local stables or cattle and chicken farms may have livestock manure for sale or free pickup. To reduce high levels of ammonia and other potent compounds in manures and to break down wood chips, compost manure for a year or two before use to mellow it.

Organic matter, nature's way of recycling fallen life into new growth, is all around. Including it in your garden enhances soil, water, and plant life.

MAKING COMPOST TEA: When added to the soil or used as a mulch, compost causes gradual improvements in soil structure and fertility. For even faster action, you can make "tea" from your compost and use it to give your garden a pick-me-up. Compost tea provides a wide array of nutrients gently diluted in a water-soluble form that plants quickly absorb and put to use.

To make compost tea, put a shovelful of compost in a fabric or cheesecloth "tea bag" and tie it closed at the top. Soak the bagged compost in a big bucket or tub of water for several days. Pull the compost out and dump it in a deserving garden, then pour the tea into a watering can. It's ideal for watering potted plants, particularly summer flowers and tropicals, and can coax heavy feeders like cucumbers and squash into growing their best.

MINIMIZING SURFACE TENSION: There are two types of soap for plants: insecticidal soaps, which kill pests, and soaps used as wetting agents, which make water penetrate dry earth and peat planting mixes more easily. Professional growers have spread this knowledge about how to make water work more efficiently to home gardeners through the gardening grapevine.

Soaps contain surfactants that alter the tension of the surface of the waters. Water molecules cohere to make pools that hold water-scooting bugs aloft as if they were skating on an invisible elastic membrane. When mixed with water, the surfactants in soap concentrate on the surface of a pool and break water bonds allowing droplets to separate and spread out. Instead of running off when it hits dry soil, water can work in more freely.

COMPOSTING FOR EVERY LIFESTYLE

It is an incontestable fact that fallen leaves, old vegetable scraps, and hay will decay. How quickly they rot and how clean the resulting organic matter will be depends on how they are composted. People in no hurry for soil amendments can compost the easy way, by dumping grass clippings, leaves, and seedless weeds in a heap. Gardeners hungry for top-quality organic matter can make compost faster and better with a managed compost pile. Compost is ready to use when the original leaves and other material become loose, dark, and unidentifiable.

Most woody and vegetable matter and livestock manures are ideal for composting. But you should avoid composting anything that poses a health risk or may contaminate the organic matter produced. *Here are some leftovers to avoid:*

- Manure from meat-eaters, including dogs and cats
- Meat or meat products
- Chemically treated plants
- Aggressive seeds or weeds, such as ground ivy or gooseneck loosestrife, that could grow in the compost pile

SIMPLE COMPOSTING

1. Find an unused corner of your property for the compost heap. You can place it behind the garage or in another out-of-the-way location, or screen it with a hedge or fence to let it work out of eyesight.
2. Pile up fallen leaves, seedless weeds, pruning leftovers, even kitchen scraps such as coffee grounds in a 3-foot square area. Avoid insect- or disease-infested material. If possible, chop up twigs and wood finely to speed its decay.
3. Continue to add to the heap until it is 3 feet high. Then begin a new pile, allowing the first pile to finish decaying, a process that can take a couple of years.
4. If you need compost before the entire pile decays, dig down to the bottom to find the oldest material, which is the first to become garden-ready.

Gardening guru Jerry Baker has long been a proponent of washing the lawn for this very reason. He has concocted plant shampoos that he says soften the soil, but in reality they are changing water to make it act wetter.

A wetting agent may be particularly helpful on grass that has a lot of thatch, matted grass roots, rhizomes, and stems that may impede water penetration. Just watering with a lot of liquid soap, however, may not

MANAGED COMPOSTING

1. Find an out-of-the-way place for the compost pile, or contain it in composting bins or barrels specially designed to speed decay and allow easy access to the organic matter.
2. For a free-form compost pile, cover the ground in a 3-foot square area with coarse sticks to make the base of the pile. The sticks will allow some air to penetrate into the pile, encouraging decomposition.
3. Gather organic matter as you work around the yard. Start with a 3-inch-deep layer of brown or dry hay, twigs, sawdust, wood shavings, or other carbon-rich leftovers. Add a layer of nitrogen-rich green vegetable debris—chemical-free grass clippings and lettuce leaves—as well as rabbit, guinea pig, or livestock manure. Continue to blend the two kinds of organic matter, making a nutrient mix that nourishes decay-causing organisms.

   Although it is preferable to include only healthy, seed-free vegetation, this is not as vital as with simple composting. This pile will heat up and destroy some of these nuisances so they cannot return to the garden.
4. When the pile gets to be 3 feet high, start a new one.
5. Use a pitchfork to fluff the compost pile as often as once a month; aerate the middle to heat up and speed up the process.
6. During dry weather, you can water the compost pile lightly to keep decomposition actively proceeding.
7. Harvest the finished compost when it is dark and loose.

OTHER METHODS

While the above are two tried-and-true composting methods, making compost is a craft that can be approached in many different ways. Instead of making a compost pile, for example, you can bury old leaves in a hole in your garden or till them into open soil at the end of the growing season. The important point is to let what came from the earth return to the earth, enriching the garden as it does.

prove productive. States such as Indiana sell only low-phosphate detergents; these can be harmful to plants. A specially formulated product, such as Baker's plant shampoos or soil conditioners that include wetting agents, beneficial bacteria, and enzymes, are safer selections. Another option is removing the thatch with aerating or dethatching equipment.

Professional growers buy commercial wetting agents, which usually are not sold at retail. Nurseries often use granular formulas that can be mixed into the potting blend, while greenhouses apply liquids in the irrigation water. In addition to improving water permeability, wetting agents allow for more uniform distribution of water and water-soluble fertilizers throughout the potting mix, producing more robust plants in a shorter time.

At home, potted plants and seedlings, especially those grown in peat-based mixes, may be moistened more effectively by adding a drop or two of mild dish soap to the watering can. They can also be transplanted into premium potting mixes that include wetting agents.

Watering a dry peat mix without a wetting agent is best done from the bottom rather than the top. Set the pot in a saucer or flat of lukewarm water and let the soil soak it up slowly until moistened throughout.

WATER-HOLDING GELS: Garden suppliers are nothing if not ingenious. Take, for example, the creation of water-holding gels, horticultural polymers that can be mixed into the soil to supply unrestricted water to roots. Water-holding gels can reduce irrigation needs by 25 to 50 percent and are ideal for gardening in dry climates. They also turn tough garden areas like small beds, pavement-encased patio and street-tree plantings, and garden pots into moist oases.

Sold under such brand names as Terrasorb, SoilMoist, and Water Works, water-holding gels can be worked into planting areas before use and watered until they swell. When added to containers, they should be premoistened and then mixed with the potting soil. Water-holding gels can make marginally well-drained soils overly wet, encouraging root rot and other diseases. After several years some of the polymers may break down into a pore-clogging slime that hinders soil aeration. They will ultimately dissolve into carbon dioxide, ammonia, water, and other benign substances.

In a Texas A & M University study, adding a water-holding gel to sandy beds of petunias (*Petunia* × *hybrida*) increased growth by up to 75 percent in dry weather. Another study found a similar response in chrysanthemums (*Dendranthema* × *grandiflorum* syn. *Chrysanthemum hortorum*). However, water-holding polymers didn't improve growth in wet weather and on more drought-tolerant flowers such as vincas (*Catharanthus roseus*) and marigolds (*Tagetes* spp.).

SELF-RELIANT PLANTINGS

A journey into the garden, with its fragrant foliage and flowers, warm earth, and small tasks that absorb the mind and body, can wipe away everyday concerns. Losing one's self in the fundamental business of creation can bring a sense of inner peace and ability to live the moment to its fullest.

When inspired by a water-conserving landscape the gardener also can be freed from certain responsibilities. Instead of being dependent on watering, the garden will be nourished by rainfall, just like plants native to the region. Wild plants rise from seedlings to towering trees using only water that falls from the skies. Species that require moisture will appear nowhere but along the banks of streams or in low damp areas of soil. Those that need sharp drainage will bloom in sandy pockets or well-drained ridges, unable to grow in soggier spots.

Taking a cue from nature, the garden landscape can be one that supports itself, or as nearly so as possible. Instead of planting a moisture-loving plant like red-twig dogwood (*Cornus alba*) beside a Scots pine (*Pinus sylvestris*), which won't tolerate wet soil, the gardener can choose

compatible companion plants and put them in sites appropriate to their
needs. New plants can be planted during seasons when rainfall will likely
be abundant—spring in the north or late fall and winter in Sacramento,
California, for instance.

But even the best-planned water-conserving landscape occasionally
will require some intervention with the hose. Watering is particularly
important if the weather becomes dry during planting time and in the
weeks or months that pass before plants become established. It cannot
be neglected in any kind of landscape.

There are ways to manage the landscape and make maximum use of
minimal water by encouraging vigorous roots, mulching, and creating
low and moderate water-use zones. A little ingenuity can go a long way
to help plants be self-sufficient.

Root Reach

Wide-spreading roots that stretch out to honeycomb the soil like
an oversized spiderweb in a forgotten corner allow a plant to
draw upon moisture reserves in the greatest possible volume of soil. Just
as a large net can catch more minnows, a wide-spreading root system can
take in more water than a small one. Roots will branch and multiply to
grow thickly where moisture and nutrients are abundant, maximizing
their absorbing potential.

In mesic, or moderately moist climates, a far-flung root system—
which on alfalfa can grow 30 feet deep and on corn 6 feet deep—is the
best insurance against damage during seasonal droughts. Rooting deeply
prepares plants such as prairie-dwelling sticky geranium (*Geranium viscosissimum*), wild potentilla (*Potentilla gracilis* subsp. *Nuttallii*), and
western hawkweed (*Hieracium Scouleri*) for finding water during a long,
hot, dry summer. In arid climates, however, foliage adapted to minimize
moisture loss can be just as important to survival as root abundance (see
page 52).

Plant roots grow according to hereditary cues of their own, but may
also respond and adapt to their surroundings. The root structure of
seedlings can determine whether plants are well suited to their environ-

ment and whether they will live or die in the place they are growing. For example, seedlings of the moisture-loving yellow birch (*Betula lutea* syn. *alleghaniensis*), have shallow roots that require even moisture to subsist. Should the soil dry out, they will perish. Seedlings of hickories (*Carya* spp.), which are found in drier uplands, immediately sink a long straight taproot deep into the soil to provide water even after the soil surface has dried.

Red maples (*Acer rubrum*), in contrast, are supremely adaptable. Where soils are deep, they will root deeply; where shallow, they will spread horizontally. This accommodating character makes red maples successful throughout their natural range, across all of the eastern and central United States. Horticulture professor Michael Dirr, in his *Manual of Woody Landscape Plants,* calls red maples a cosmopolitan species, adapted to bottomlands, swamps, forests, and rocky uplands. Their success is at least partly due to the adaptable root system.

Roots may also change from a taproot into a shallower fibrous root system if the root is pruned or kept pot-bound in the nursery. This is commonly the case with parsley seedlings, which develop deeper roots, although maturing much more slowly, from direct-sown seeds.

Roots reach their maximum potential when given prime growing conditions. Most important, the soil must be deep and loose, allowing for good drainage and aeration. Where it is dense, dry, wet, or compacted, most roots, even of naturally deep-growing species, will not grow. They will be forced to compete for resources in the top 36 inches of soil, the surface of which is precariously prone to drying out when drought strikes. Roots may have difficulty penetrating the walls of holes dug in stiff clay, which suppresses their spread and limits self-sufficiency.

Healthy, thriving plants strike a balance between root and shoot growth, each of which must be of a size that will benefit the other. Roots nourished by photosynthesis in the shoots and leaves provide aboveground portions of the plant with water, minerals, and growth hormones such as cytokinins and gibberellins that encourage cell division and shoot elongation. A large root system can supply more of these vital substances, allowing for more shoot growth, which in turn increases food production in a self-promoting cycle.

Understanding the importance of roots and encouraging them to reach out in the soil is a significant part of water-efficient gardening.

TIPS FOR SELF-RELIANT PLANTINGS

Pampering landscape plants, except for those needing evenly moist soil (see page 35), is not only unnecessary but also inadvisable. It is better for plants to stretch their roots wide across a garden bed than to linger, like a bird in a cage, in a confined area of man-made moisture. Modifying the landscape site and watering specifically to encourage self-sufficiency, as described in the section that follows, can pay dividends in water conservation for decades to come.

Plant Sparsely. Reduce demands on soil moisture reserves by spacing plants slightly farther apart than ordinarily required. This gives their roots exclusive water rights. Avoid the temptation to interplant by putting young trees in the lawn or annual flowers around a new shrub. Instead, mulch open areas to conserve moisture.

Break up Shallow Soil. If the garden soil is not naturally deep and loose (and few are), break up lower layers of soil to allow roots to sink deep (see page 38).

Plant in Beds. Where soils are heavy clay, amend and improve the soil in an entire bed, to provide a large space for free rooting. Shrubs, trees, perennials, and even annuals will have the entire expanse for rooting instead of being confined to a small hole imprisoned in unamended clay.

Soil Surfacing. Gardeners should forget what they have learned about keeping the garden neat and level. Adding some natural-looking undulations to the surface of a well-drained soil can

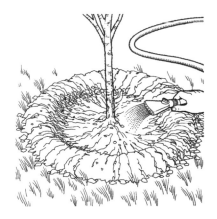

A watering basin will contain water and help it drain directly to the roots below.

encourage water to pool in strategic areas such as individual planting sites or entire landscape beds. Soil saucers and sunken beds will hold rain and irrigation water and funnel it down to plant roots directly below instead of allowing it to run off. Both can also be watered with an extension of a roof downspout to increase the amount of rainfall available.

For newly planted nursery stock, let the outer edge of the soil saucer be at or beyond the dripline, the horticultural term for the outer tips of the branches. This is the area where most active rooting takes place and where moisture will be used most readily.

In an arid-climate vegetable garden, sunken planting rows will improve water accessibility and shield crops from drying sun and wind. In moist climates, however, raised planting rows may be more effective. They provide better drainage and increase the depth of the topsoil for more extensive rooting.

Avoid Steep Slopes. While a gentle water-directing slope is good, a steep slope encourages water to run off rapidly instead of sinking in, keeping the soil below dry. If possible, make a gentle slope by changing the grade of your yard or even terracing it with a single or a series of retaining walls, building the soil into level planting beds behind them.

Water Deeply. When watering larger established plants—deep-rooting trees, shrubs, roses, peonies, and prairie natives, for instance—water long enough to moisten the soil at least 8 inches deep and preferably a foot. If in doubt, dig down in an open area of soil and see how low the water has seeped. This encourages roots to dig down, expanding their ability to absorb water, particularly during drought.

Shallow-rooted plants, such as seedlings and bluegrass lawns, on the other hand, are not naturally inclined to root deeply. They need to be watered more frequently and shallowly—to a depth of 4 to 8 inches.

Allow Some Plants to Go Dormant. Turf, old-fashioned bleeding heart (*Dicentra spectabilis*), daffodils (*Narcissus* spp.), tulips (*Tulipa* spp.), crocus (*Crocus* spp.), and other spring-blooming bulbs can fall dormant before or during drought, resting quietly until rainy weather returns or the spring season comes again. Avoid fertilizing or other procedures that stimulate new growth.

Spring-blooming annuals like pansies (*Viola* × *wittrockiana*), pot marigolds (*Calendula officinalis*), and sweet alyssum (*Lobularia mar-*

PLANTING TREES AND SHRUBS

To give new trees and shrubs the best possible chance to quickly develop wide-spreading, self-supporting roots, take care to plant them properly. A good start is particularly important for large woody plants, permanent landscape fixtures that will spend the remainder of their lives in the site you have provided.

1. Buy healthy trees and shrubs with large, full root balls. Have the nursery deliver a heavy plant right to your planting hole rather than risk your back or the plant by attempting to move it yourself.

2. Select a tree or shrub that can thrive in the sun and soil conditions in your yard. While it is possible to amend an unpromising soil in and around the planting hole, you want the roots of trees and shrubs to grow far and wide and need a congenial native soil for that to happen.

3. Dig a planting hole in a garden bed or lawn area, making the hole one and a half times as wide as the root ball, but no deeper than the root ball. The firm hole base keeps the plant from sinking too low in soft soil. In heavy soil, you can make the hole only two-thirds as deep as the root ball, building up a well-aerated raised bed around the protruding upper portion of the root ball.

   Carve the sides of the hole slightly deeper than the center of the hole, inviting the growing roots to spread out into the surrounding soil. In heavy soils, lightly score the sides of the hole with the tip of a shovel or a garden fork to make them loose and easy for roots to penetrate. Use good garden soil to fill the hole, not old pieces of turf or subsoil clay.

itima) can fade naturally, leaving openings for new plants. Consider drought-inspired dormancy or death a natural occurrence, which it is, and revel in the diversity and change it will inspire.

Seal Leaves to Minimize Transpiration. Before drought strikes, apply an antitranspirant, a product that seals leaf surfaces to minimize losses from evapotranspiration. This is a great way to protect broad leaf evergreens during winter, when the soil is frozen and water lost from the leaves cannot be replaced.

4. Remove a container-grown tree and shrub from its pot, loosen any tangled, matted, or winding roots you find on the perimeter of the root mass, and then set it in the hole.

   Put a balled-and-burlapped tree or shrub (a plant with roots protected in the fabric-covered root ball) into the planting hole with its roots still covered. Once properly in place, cut off all twine and as much burlap as possible to prevent future damage to the trunk or roots.

   Double-check the plant's placement in the hole: first lay the handle of a shovel or a yard-stick across the top of the hole. The soil surface should be level with the top of the roots, unless you are creating a raised bed, in which case the roots will protrude. Step back and make sure any tree trunks are straight upright, shifting the roots if needed to get the trunk upright.

5. Fill the hole gradually, letting a hose trickle in as you do so to wet the entire planting from the bottom up. Water helps soil settle around the roots, leaving no dry air pockets to hinder root growth. Lightly firm the soil occasionally with the back of a hoe or your foot.

6. Stop filling the hole once it is an inch below the surrounding soil to leave a concave watering basin. Encircle the planting hole with a low mound of soil, about 3 inches high and 3 inches wide. It will naturally catch rainwater and funnel it to the young roots. During dry weather, you can let a hose drizzle in the basin.

7. Cover the planting area with mulch, such as shredded bark or bark chips. This will help keep the soil moist and discourage the growth of weeds or grass, which compete with tree and shrub roots and can significantly slow growth and establishment.

Antitranspirants, coincidentally, also can discourage leaf diseases like powdery mildew on perennials such as phlox (*Phlox paniculata*) and bee balm (*Monarda* spp.) and vegetables such as cucumbers and tomatoes.

Wilt-Pruf, a pine oil that dries into a thin water-preserving film, should be sprayed on the top and bottom of the leaf. It must be applied in daylight with temperatures above freezing, which requires planning ahead when using it on rhododendrons (*Rhododendron* spp.) and mountain laurels (*Kalmia latifolia*) in winter.

Slow Winds. Cut the speed and strength of blustery winds which, like indoor hot air vents, will draw moisture from both leaves and soil. Putting a windbreak between the garden and the prevailing winds can help in windblown locations. In general, a windbreak reduces the velocity of the wind for a distance as much as five times its height, or 100 feet for a 20-foot-tall hedge or 20 feet for a 4-foot-tall hedge.

Staggered rows of durable evergreens, such as limber and Austrian pines (*Pinus flexilis* and *Pinus nigra*), slow the wind year-round, including winter. Deciduous trees and shrubs will cut the wind during the growing season, keeping tall asters (*Aster* spp.), delphiniums (*Delphinium* spp.), and hollyhocks (*Alcea rosea*) from being blown down. Fences and masonry walls, unlike hedges, begin working instantly and need no time to grow. A pretty and functional alternative is lattice planted with vines.

REDUCE EVAPORATION FROM POTTED PLANTS

When growing container plants, reduce evaporative losses by putting smaller pots inside larger ones and filling the space between with moist vermiculite. Line permeable containers, such as wood or clay, with plastic. Mulch the open soil on top of the pot with compost or bark. Choose low, broad pots, which lose less irrigation water to gravity, over tall, slim pots.

Minimize Sun. Sun, like wind, accelerates evaporation and drying of soil and plant alike. (Just put a flat of annual seedlings on a porch where the sun peeks through. Seedlings baked in the sun will wilt within hours while those left in the shade will remain moist and perky.)

Where the sun is intense, gardening in the shade of a building, wall, arbor, or pergola will reduce water needs. Even plants that prefer full sun can benefit from light shade in the heat of the afternoon in warm climates. The shady spot under shallow-rooted trees like Norway maples (*Acer platanoides*) and American beeches (*Fagus grandifolia*) will suffer from root competition and be unlikely to provide the same kind of moist sanctuary.

SEPARATING PLANTS ACCORDING TO WATER USE

The same resourcefulness that has made irrigation easy allows contemporary gardeners to plan a landscape that needs little irrigation. The traditional practice of grouping plants according to their preference for sun or shade can be expanded to include coupling plants by moisture needs—making landscape zones of low, medium, and high water requirements. The success of this method in arid western states confirms *Horticulture Magazine* and *Victory Garden* contributor Roger Swain's comments that planning is more important than plumbing.

In dry weather, gardeners might water twice a week to provide even moisture to tomatoes and potatoes. Gardens of drought-tolerant plants like lavender (*Lavandula* spp.) and rosemary (*Rosmarinus officinalis*), herbs that insist on sharp drainage, might never need watering once established. Separating plants such as these into different landscape zones eliminates the need to water the entire landscape, whether it needs it or not, and permits watering just the thirsty sections, which saves water, time, and money.

Depending on the climate, the size of high- and low-water-use areas can vary. Drought-tolerant plants can be emphasized in dry climates and areas with water bans or ticklish wells likely to run precariously low in dry weather. Dry zones are ideal for slopes, rocky or sandy soils, areas beyond where the hose easily stretches, or the parched strip under rain-blocking roof overhangs, which can be as dry as a desert. Plants requiring moderate moisture levels can prevail in mesic regions, such as the Midwest and East Coast, with more-or-less regular rainfall.

Areas of highest water use—a bluegrass lawn or rose garden—can be conveniently located near the house, where water is most accessible. This kind of planning will spare gardeners the nuisance of dragging hoses across the yard for years to come. Better yet, these gardens could be provided with an automatic irrigation system that eliminates the time and trouble involved with manual watering.

A ZONED LANDSCAPE: A water-zoned landscape is illustrated on page 57. The front entryway garden, which borders the hot driveway, stretching under the eaves next to the house and forming beds that brighten the front walk and front door, is a low-moisture zone. Designed for all-season color, dried ornamental grasses and evergreen junipers hold winter interest. For spring flowers, this garden uses Crusader hawthorn (*Crataegus crus-galli* 'Crusader'), which may need occasional watering, and daffodils, which take advantage of spring showers and then go dormant for the dry summer. Drought-tolerant annuals and perennials, such as California poppies (*Eschscholzia californica*), moss rose (*Portulaca grandiflora*), yarrow (*Achillea* spp.), coneflowers (*Rudbeckia* spp.), and coreopsis (*Coreopsis* spp.), bloom from summer into fall.

Behind the house, surrounding the patio, is an area of moderate water use composed of plants that can live in some dry soil but benefit from occasional soaking during extended dry weather. A honey locust (*Gleditsia triacanthos* var. *inermis*) shades the patio and provides a backdrop of greenery for the house. The patio is edged by an informal grouping of spring-flowering Mohican viburnum (*Viburnum lantana* 'Mohican'), which continue to bring color to the landscape with their red summer fruit.

An enclosed vegetable garden, located just outside the kitchen door and adjacent to the patio, includes tomatoes, peppers, lettuce, and other plants that grow best in evenly moist soil. The lawn, another high-water area located nearby, also will need regular watering if it is to remain green during dry weather.

PLANNING A
WATER-EFFICIENT GARDEN

When summer is high and the ground is dry, gardeners are likely to be most aware of the need for irrigation. However, this is not the time to change the landscape to make it more water-efficient. Provide as much water as your plants need now, helping them abide summer droughts, and start planning so you won't have to use so much water next year. There is no better time to watch which plants thrive despite heat and drought—they will be ideal candidates for low-water areas of the yard. Note which plants can't last more than a couple of days without a drink from the hose—they will be good

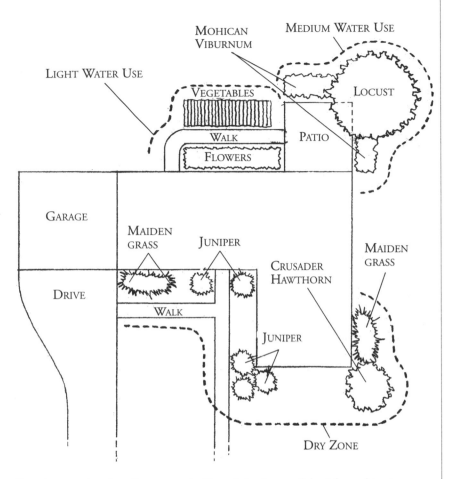

LIGHT WATER USE

MOHICAN
VIBURNUM

MEDIUM WATER USE

VEGETABLES

LOCUST

WALK

PATIO

FLOWERS

GARAGE

MAIDEN
GRASS

JUNIPER

CRUSADER
HAWTHORN

MAIDEN
GRASS

DRIVE

WALK

JUNIPER

DRY ZONE

Drawing a garden plan allows easy reshuffling of plantings until the right combinations emerge. Dividing the landscape into water-use zones makes for easy maintenance.

candidates for a water-intensive part of the garden or for maneuvering out of the landscape altogether.

To begin planning in an organized way, use a pencil and paper to make a landscape plan suitable for sketching and reshuffling all your ideas until the right plan emerges. The best way to start is with a scale drawing of your yard, or of the garden you want to make more water-efficient. Plot plans, architectural blueprints, or previous landscape plans can provide the layout of your yard. If you can't find any of these, measure the length and width of the property and the house, plus any landscape features you want to keep, including large trees, patios, and bed contours. Sketch it all to scale on a piece of graph paper.

Drawing the plan to scale is vital for the accuracy and usefulness of the sketch. Many landscape designers use the scale 4 feet = 1 inch, meaning 4 feet of actual yard space will take up 1 inch on the plan. Because some graph paper breaks down each inch into five or ten small squares, 5 feet = 1 inch can be an easier way to begin. To get a lot of detail in a single garden, you might want to use 2 feet = 1 inch. Write the scale you have selected on the plan so you can refer to it as you do future design work.

When measuring the yard, use a measuring tape or, better yet, a measuring wheel, a tool popular among professional landscapers. Holding on to a telescoping handle, you roll the wheel through the yard, letting it calculate the distance you travel. Estimating distances, with a guess or a stride, seldom provides precise results.

Include an arrow that points north on the plan and offers hints at which sites will be most sun-drenched, hot, and dry. Gardens located in open areas or to the south of buildings or walls will have a full day of sunshine and, as a consequence, will experience the most evaporation. Gardens on the north side of buildings and walls will be shaded and protected from the sun, staying cooler and moister than gardens with southern exposures. Gardens with eastern exposures feel the morning sun but are sheltered from hotter afternoon sun common to western exposures.

Even more information about moisture conditions can be gleaned from varying soil and topography conditions. Areas on slopes, under gutters, beneath shallow rooted shade trees, in the midst of paving, or on sandy soils all are likely to remain on the dry side. Low parts of the yard, where water will accumulate, and areas of rich clay soil will tend to stay moister.

You may also want to pencil in notations about which parts of the yard will be easiest to water and therefore good candidates for moisture-loving plants. If you don't want to drag a hose more than about 25 feet, keep water-loving plants within 25 feet of the house and plan to use drought-tolerant plants in gardens that are farther out.

A practical landscape plan should include more than plants and gardens. You should map out any existing utilities—underground gas and cable television lines or invisible dog fencing—that you don't want to damage by digging in the vicinity. You can sketch in future utility needs as well—electric lines for night lighting or water lines for garden irrigation. Note the position of overhead power lines as well, making sure they don't get entangled with trees or tall shrubs you might be thinking about growing nearby.

To make the yard most useful, create bubble diagrams, or circles showing spaces of varying uses such as a private hedge-enclosed reading area, children's play equipment in a space that can be watched from the house, or a convenient spot for barbecuing on pleasant summer nights. Then you can plan landscape structures and plantings that will cater to the intended use of each space.

These areas will also need hardscape—walks, walls, patios, and other built structures—which you should draw in on the plan. Hardscape should be the first landscape element to be installed, and its position will be vital to all future planning.

When you get down to the nitty-gritty of where to place particular plants, use tracing paper overlays set atop the master plan, since this part of the process could undergo a lot of revision. This way you don't have to erase each new idea, but can begin anew and still consult your previous ideas.

Free your artistic side when planning for interesting color and foliage throughout the seasons and satisfying design principles such as balance, rhythm, and focal point. You can find good design books at libraries, or consult a landscape designer to explore and incorporate these elements into your plan.

When sketching in the plants you want to include, give them enough space to mature, both horizontally and vertically. Consult good garden books and catalogs to determine the ultimate dimensions of the misleadingly petite, young plants found in most nurseries.

To help make the plan jump from the two-dimensional paper to three-dimensional real life, you can use stakes and string or the curving line of a garden hose to envision how landscape beds, paths, and other potential garden structures will look in the yard. To go a step further, set items of a similar size—barrels, beanbag chairs, coat racks—to imagine how the scheme will look.

Once you're satisfied with your landscape plan, you can use it to make shopping lists of the plants you need. You can shop for everything at once and possibly get a better price with a big order. Or if the potential costs are prohibitive, you could buy the most important plants this year and save the rest for later.

You may decide to move some of your perennials, herbs, or other smaller plants. Make a note of where you want them to go, but wait to move them until the best planting and transplanting season arrives.

In northern climates, where winter can be a furious season, spring is the safest planting time for most hardy plants. Planting during this cool and usually moist season in the eastern and central United States and also in western areas such as Casper, Wyoming, and Great Falls, Montana, allows for vigorous root growth before the arrival of summer and, beyond that, winter.

Late summer or early fall is the second most popular planting and transplanting time for northern climates. Although prone to drought in some areas, this second planting season allows hardy plants to become established before winter becomes frigidly cold. New transplants, however, will probably need water, sometimes a lot of it.

In southern climates, where summer heat can be stressful for new plants, you may want to plant in fall or late winter. Although the temperature varies among cold, cool, and quite warm in Atlanta, Georgia, from December to May, the precipitation averages more than 4 inches of rain a month. If nature is kind, you may not need to water new plantings much or at all. In arid areas like El Paso, Texas, which have little rain in fall and winter, extra irrigation cannot be avoided.

The relatively mild and moist weather common in the Pacific Northwest makes it a planter's paradise. In Seattle, Washington, and Portland, Oregon, for instance, rainfall tends to be abundant from fall into early spring, allowing gardeners to pick a convenient planting time.

Farther south, where the West Coast transforms into a dry Mediterranean climate, cities like Sacramento, California, experience several inches of rain a month from November through March. This is the time to plant, before rainfall drops to a dribble from June through September.

If in doubt about the rainfall patterns in your area, ask a local botan-

ROARING '20S MULCHES

While some mulching materials may be new and improved, the process of mulching is classic. In *The Practical Book of Outdoor Flowers,* published in 1924, Richardson Wright suggested mulching roses with tobacco stems, which contain the natural pesticide nicotine, to deter aphids. He also recommended changing to grass clippings in July and August to deter weeds and save soil moisture.

ical garden or Cooperative Extension Service horticulturist. You can usually find the Cooperative Extension Service listed under federal or county government in the Yellow or Blue Pages.

MINIMIZING LAWN: To stay green, lawn grasses need a regular supply of moisture as well as labor-intensive mowing while actively growing. Turf is among the most water-hungry elements of the landscape, which raises the question, Is having a big lawn worth the effort? Many people say yes, because they see the lawn as more than a mere landscape element. Lawns increase property values, provide play space, and, with regular mowing, make a homeowner look like a good neighbor. These social connections make lawns hard to eliminate altogether.

Restricting turf to save water has resulted in some dramatic efforts to reduce the monopoly that lawns have on most landscapes. For example, in January 1997, the Reno, Nevada, Water Board tried to ban turf from new commercial landscapes and slopes steeper than 10 degrees. They also requested that multitenant developments allow no more than 25 percent of the landscape to be carpeted in turf. But the landscape industry balked at these sweeping restrictions, preferring to limit landscape watering to two days a week rather than prohibit turf in some areas.

Shaving the size of a lawn is an easily accepted alternative, and it often reduces landscape maintenance and water waste. Shapely perimeter beds of easy-care ground covers or clusters of shrubs and trees can replace lawn and create a more interesting and environmentally harmonious landscape. Ground covers are also good substitutes for lawn in out-of-the-way places, such as narrow side yards, slivers of ground beside fences and walks, and shady areas under trees.

Another option for new homes or lawns undergoing renovation is to replace lusty bluegrass with more drought-tolerant grass species. One little-known contender is buffalo grass (*Buchloe dactyloides*), which naturally grows only 4 to 8 inches tall, seldom needs mowing, and requires only 10 to 15 inches of water a year. A plant of the short-grass prairies, it is green in the growing season and tan in the winter. A deep-rooted companion grass, suitable for seed mixtures, is blue grama grass (*Bouteloua gracilis*). It can grow from 6 to 24 inches high with as little as

10 to 15 inches of water a year. Another choice is tall fescue (*Festuca arundinacea*), a more traditional and especially deep-rooted lawn grass that can tolerate as little as 18 inches of water a year.

In comparison, Kentucky bluegrass (*Poa* spp.), bent grass (*Agrostis* spp.), and carpet grass lawns are among the least tolerant of dry soils, needing as much as 45 inches of water a year. Ryegrasses (*Lolium* spp.), St. Augustine grass (*Stenotaphrum* spp.), and Redtop (*Agrostis* spp.) are only slightly more drought tolerant.

When changing lawn dynamics won't work, a water-conserving gardener can irrigate more efficiently using the following suggestions.

• Wait to water until the surface of the ground is dry and grass begins to lie flat when underfoot. This prewilting condition will occur first in areas of full sun or dry slopes.

• When watering is necessary, soak the soil 6 to 8 or even 12 inches deep, encouraging grasses to grow deeper roots. To determine how deeply the water has penetrated, slice into newly watered turf with a shovel, unearthing a cross section. If irrigation has not seeped to below the roots—encouraging them to stretch downward—plan to water more, possibly in two sessions (see page 51).

• Add a soil conditioner with a wetting agent to the lawn before watering (see page 43).

• Extend roof downspouts to send rainwater out into the lawn.

• Water lawns slowly enough so that the moisture will be fully absorbed without running off. For clay soil, which soaks up water sluggishly, this can mean providing ¼ inch of water two to three times a day, as often as twice a week.

• If an extended drought becomes critical, allow the lawn to go without water and fertilizer. It will fall dormant for up to 6 weeks. Beyond this period, watering deeply every 3 weeks will help prevent the lawn from dying altogether. It's best to avoid heavy foot traffic during this time.

• Water when the sun is low in the early morning to minimize evaporative losses of irrigation water. The evening is also an efficient time to water, with one exception. Lavishly irrigated lawns may be prone to fungal diseases encouraged by moisture lingering on grass blades, crowns, and roots in the cool of the evening.

• Allow the lawn to get long and luxurious; the self-shading blades reduce water loss and encourage deeper rooting.

MULCHING TO MINIMIZE
MOISTURE LOSS

The word *mulch,* signifying "soft" or "yielding," originated in Middle English; by the era of Early Modern English, its meaning evolved to "rotten hay." This definition may conjure foul connotations, but it is sweet to the experienced gardener, who knows the incomparable value of organic material for the soil. From these humble beginnings, mulch has risen to a place of high esteem. It is credited in many circles with the growing popularity of low-maintenance landscaping.

Mulch, a soil-covering coating of organic or inorganic material such as bark, compost, or pebbles, reduces water evaporation, cutting the need for watering by up to 50 percent. However, even mulched gardens will need to be watered deeply from time to time. Shallow sprinkles during dry weather moisten only the mulch and soil surface, encouraging shallow root growth and minimizing drought tolerance.

By covering barren earth, mulch also suppresses weeds. Nature never leaves open soil alone for long, gobbling it up with quick-colonizing weeds such as chicory, dandelions, crabgrass, and pigweed. A coating of mulch can keep the soil dark and uninviting for these opportunists.

The porous nature of mulches made of bark, pine needles, straw, and other coarse-textured materials reduces the velocity of rainfall by slamming on the brakes so that water can enter the work zone of the soil in a slow and steady pace. This allows it to soak in deeply instead of careening off and running into nearby ditches and streams. By doing the tough work—enforcing the slow speed zone—mulch keeps the soil from getting compressed, compacted, and crusted. It encourages conditions ideal for root growth. Fine-textured mulches such as grass clippings are likely to compress into a tight mat under an onslaught of heavy rain, however, providing little advantage.

By covering fallen leaves that are infected, mulches help slow the spread of diseases like black spot, whose spores are carried in bouncing raindrops to healthy leaves. Beds of straw and other mulches can shield ground-hugging fruit like melons and pumpkins from rot-causing pathogens in the soil.

Like an earthen blanket, mulch moderates temperature changes in the soil; this increases root comfort zones, allowing prolonged root growth in hot or cold climates or areas prone to rapid and extreme temperature changes. When applied in summer, organic mulch keeps the soil cooler. Applied in late fall after the soil is frozen, it discourages the repeated thawing and refreezing that causes soil shifting and possible root damage. When applied in spring, organic mulch keeps soil cool to delay bloom and minimize frost damage to bulbs, fruit trees, and perennials. As organic mulches decompose, they provide the soil with organic matter that can improve its structure (see page 65).

Plastic mulches trap solar heat and can speed the warming of vegetable garden soil to allow for early planting. Clear plastic mulch used in the heat of summer superheats the soil, killing weed seedlings.

Mulch is not perfect for every garden, however. It can only be used on well-drained soil; it makes any poorly drained soil even wetter. If applied too thickly, it can smother the soil by hindering air penetration or provide a fertile environment for surface rooting, which is perhaps the most water-inefficient situation of all. It can also house slugs, snails, mice, and other pests who feed on plants placed conveniently nearby.

Mulch may have little to offer drought-tolerant plants from arid regions, particularly when used in an irrigated landscape. A Texas Tech University study of Southwestern shrub species cliff rose (*Cowania mexicana* var. *Stansburiana*), curl-leaf mahogany (*Cercocarpus ledifolius*), desert olive (*Forestiera neomexicana*), Apache plume (*Fallugia paradoxa*), and winter fat (*Ceratoides lanata*) showed 3-inch and 6-inch-deep layers of bark mulch made no difference in growth or lifespan during the 18 months after planting.

MULCHES: ORGANIC AND INORGANIC: Mulch, which once had to be gleaned from nearby farm fields or agricultural industries, now

---

MULCH IS COOL

The ability of mulch to moderate heat can reduce the transpiration rate of trees, thereby saving moisture. Street trees planted in openings in hot asphalt, which can be 20 to 25° C. warmer than turf or mulch, may lose one-third more water than trees planted in mulched earth or turf. In an arid climate, however, trees planted in asphalt lose *less* water than those grown in turf or mulch because they close their stomata longer, which does not bode well for growth.

has become a big home-gardening business. Many kinds can be purchased, including year-old leaf mold, mushroom compost, cocoa-bean hulls, and crushed rocks of many hues. Specially engineered landscape fabrics and papers, underpinnings that make decorative mulches work more effectively, can be added to a shopping list. To be a wise consumer, a gardener needs to know the pros and cons of each product and to decide which will be most beneficial for his or her own garden.

Organic mulches such as shredded bark, bark chunks, and straw break down after a year or two in the garden, adding essential organic matter to the soil and requiring regular replacement. Woody mulches consume nitrogen as they decay, so much so that they can slow the growth of nearby plants unless extra fertilizer is added as a supplement.

For this reason, some gardeners prefer to mulch with compost—rich, dark weed-free leaf mold or mushroom compost. This predigested organic matter offers the best of both worlds: it adds nutrients to the earth while improving soil structure. Compost also reduces evaporation and increases water permeability, but it is not especially efficient in limiting weeds. Its loose texture, however, makes compost easy to run a hoe through, so you can uproot weeds standing up instead of having to stoop to pull them up by hand.

Inorganic mulches, such as gravel, plastic, and brick chunks, add an aura of permanence but don't break down like organic mulches do, so they give little or nothing to the soil. Bright white pebbles or red or green plastic dazzle the eye more than the ordinary earth tones of organic mulches, which may make the inorganic kind more desirable for appearance-conscious gardeners.

Here are the pros and cons of some common mulches.

Aluminum Foil. Although expensive, aluminum foil can be used under aphid-prone plants, such as squash and Chinese cabbage, to confuse and deter the pests. It can be combined with trickle irrigation for easy-care gardening.

Bark. Readily available in bags or by the bushel or truckload, bark comes in coarse-textured chunks or finer-textured shredded or double-shredded slivers. You can choose from rot-resistant redwood or cypress bark or other barks that may be partly decayed. Use care when mulching with bark bought in bulk. Bark stockpiled in a big heap in a soil yard may suffer anaerobic decomposition, becoming acidic and burning plants when applied.

Cocoa-bean Hulls. A by-product of chocolate making, this mulch has the same candy bar smell as the air over Hershey, Pennsylvania. Dark and attractive, the hulls are good to use on beds of smaller plants; however, their aroma is occasionally accused of attracting rodents. Because cocoa-bean hulls are not only fine textured but also expensive, limit layers to no more than 2 inches deep.

Landscape Paper. Biodegradable black landscape paper made specifically for use as a mulch is available in rolls 24 and 48 inches wide. Unroll the paper across a bed, anchoring the edges with soil, stones, boards, or metal pins. Cut holes in it for vegetables, annuals, even shrubs. For ornamental beds, cover the paper with decorative mulch. In vegetable gardens, the dark paper can work solo, absorbing solar warmth. Most brands decay after the growing season is through.

Under the premise that two mulches are better than one, gardeners have long underlaid their decorative mulches with newspaper to provide extra protection against weeds and water loss. Paper allows air and water to penetrate and decays to add organic matter to the ground. A layer several sheets thick will hold for a growing season, but using a thicker layer is not advisable. A recent study at Auburn University found that a ½-inch-deep mulch of ground paper pellets (recycled primarily from newsprint, with a few magazines and telephone books thrown in) severely reduced the growth of shallow-rooted annuals—marigolds (*Tagetes* spp.), salvia (*Salvia* spp.), geraniums (*Pelargonium* × *hortorum*), and ageratums (*Ageratum Houstonianum*)—grown in acidic soil. Aluminum that leached out of the paper prevented plants from absorbing phosphorus, a nutrient essential for growth.

Landscape Fabric. This product has become the darling of the landscape industry, replacing black plastic. Because it is porous, it allows air and water to pass in and out, which encourages healthy soil conditions. When combined with a topping of organic mulch, it is among the most efficient ways to suppress weeds. After a few years, when the topping begins to harbor weeds, the mulch can be swept back and the landscape fabric flipped over for a fresh start. Landscape fabrics work best with large, immobile plants and lack the flexibility needed for perennial, annual, and herb gardens.

Most landscape fabrics are made of polypropylene or polyester and come in rolls 3 or 4 feet wide. They are also available in squares that are handy for mulching under trees and shrubs.

While inexpensive landscape fabrics last for only one year, top quality brands are guaranteed for more than five years, and some stay on the job for twenty years before beginning to decay. One brand comes with an underlying layer of capillary matting that helps keep the soil below moist.

Leaves. Nature mulches her deciduous woodlands with fallen leaves, and gardeners can do the same in informal beds. Leaves break down to provide everything woody plants need to grow—organic material and a complete range of nutrients. Do not apply leaves in a thick layer; they may mat and form a barrier impenetrable to water and air. For an airier mulch, chop

EARTH AS MULCH

One early form of mulch nearly forgotten today is the earth itself, which was shallowly cultivated and called dust mulch. Although not as effective as organic or inorganic mulches, broken-up soil clumps can act as an evaporation-slowing soil covering that, when kept loose, also allows water to penetrate deep into the soil.

"However contradictory it may sound, it is true that a mulch of dry dust lying on top of the soil will preserve the dampness underneath better than a soil that has been left to bake and cake in the hot sun," wrote Richardson Wright in *The Practical Book of Outdoor Flowers.*

and mix leaves with straw, or compost them and mulch with leaf mold. Most leaf mulches are applied in fall, when they are readily available, and can be tilled into the soil in spring or topped with a more decorative mulch.

Pine Needles. Usually shed in spring, pine needles make an outstanding loose mulch for conifers, rhododendrons, and other acid-loving plants. Although it takes a lot of pine trees to collect a quantity of needles, they break down slowly and don't require frequent replacement.

Plastic. When laid over garden beds and cut to allow insertion of plants, rolls of plastic eliminate problems with weeds, which makes them popular. Plastic forms a water-tight cover that holds in soil moisture but limits rewetting later in the season. In areas prone to drought, underlaying plastic mulch with trickle irrigation lines is the best way to provide a regular moisture supply.

Without evaporation to dry the soil surface, plants grown in plastic-mulched beds may root shallowly, which is counterproductive for long-lived trees and shrubs in particular, so these plants are best grown without

VEGETABLE GARDENING WITH PLASTIC MULCH

Plastic mulch is the key to an easy-care garden of vining plants such as tomatoes, squash, pumpkins, or melons, or a bed of strawberries, or large single-vegetable plants such as peppers and eggplants. It holds in moisture, prevents weed growth, and keeps vines neatly and cleanly off the ground. It is also easy to use. Here's how:

1. Buy plastic garden mulch of a width and length appropriate for the garden space you have in mind. A rectangular space the width of the plastic usually works best.
2. Prepare the soil well by tilling and removing weeds, then adding organic matter, fertilizer, and any other amendments crops might need now or later. Remember, you won't have a chance to work the soil again this year. You can also lay soaker

hoses or drip irrigation on the soil surface to make it easy to water during dry weather (see pages 89 and 95).

3. Spread the plastic over the prepared bed, securing the edges to the ground with earth staples, rocks, or boards.
4. Cut holes in the plastic with scissors or a knife wherever you want to put plants; try to avoid damaging water lines below. Set in transplants or seeds and water well.
5. You may need to pull a few weeds out of the planting holes as summer goes on. If weeds are close to crop plants, cut the weeds off rather than risk uprooting the crop as you pull or damaging its roots. To fertilize, water with a liquid product, which can be absorbed not only by the foliage but also by the roots if applied through the planting hole.

plastic mulch. In response to this problem, some plastic mulches have been reformulated to let air and water flow through; for example, one brand is perforated with millions of tiny holes. Plastic mulches come in a variety of colors that produce different effects in the garden. Black plastic, the standard, allows no light to penetrate, which discourages the germination of most weed seeds. It is popular in vegetable gardens, where its use minimizes weeding around squash, pumpkins, and strawberries. Black plastic absorbs solar heat and can increase soil temperatures below it by 5 or more degrees.

When it comes to warming the soil, dark green infrared-transmitting plastic mulch is even better than black. It allows solar warmth to penetrate through the plastic to the soil as if the mulch was clear but blocks the wavelengths of light that encourage weed sprouting.

Plastic mulches of other colors, such as red plastic used under tomatoes, may increase productivity or confuse pests and hinder their feeding. Research into the possibilities is ongoing.

Stone. For a bright or contemporary look, many gardeners turn to white, red, or gray stone mulches of gravel, crushed marble or limestone, or volcanic rocks. These mulches will not decay, but may sink down into the soil and require replenishing every few years. If allowed to roll into the lawn, stones can bump heads with mower blades and nearby windows, dogs, and kids. Weeds and self-sowing flowers may get started in a stone cover and require weeding.

Straw. This inexpensive and rustic-looking mulch is a champion for a vegetable garden or working cut-flower garden. It also can help keep a newly sown lawn moist. A 4- to 6-inch-deep mulch usually lasts through

COMMON MULCHES IN A NUTSHELL

Shredded Bark and Wood Chips	organic; attractive; moderate weed suppression; uses nitrogen to decay; speed of decay accelerates with diminishing particle size
Straw	organic; moderate weed suppression; nondecorative for new lawn or kitchen garden; can harbor animal nests
Landscape Paper	organic; efficient temporary weed suppression; requires coverage with decorative mulch in ornamental beds
Landscape Fabric	inorganic; porous; moderate to good weed suppression when combined with organic mulch; best used under a few larger plants
Plastic	inorganic; nonporous; efficient weed suppression; best for strawberries and vegetables; varying colors can speed growth, heat soil, and discourage pests; can encourage shallow rooting
Gravel	won't decay; encourages surface drainage; minimal to moderate weed suppression; can be bright and eye-attracting

the growing season. When no longer needed, it can be tilled into the ground to decay. Be sure to buy seed-free straw, not hay, which comes with weeds and seeds.

Wood Chips. Generally quite coarse-textured, wood chips last longer in the garden than shredded bark. They can be purchased bagged or in bulk. Thrifty consumers may even be able to talk arborists, municipalities, or electric utility companies into donating the wood chips made after trimming trees. As they decay, wood chips absorb nitrogen from the soil, so your garden may need an extra dose of fertilizer to keep it growing well.

APPLICATION DEPTHS AND TIMING: Mulching need not be a spring-only event that begins when convenience stores sprout piles of bagged shredded cypress. The slogan "Timing Is Everything" applies to mulching as well as business, and deciding when to mulch depends on the goal of mulching.

To suppress weeds, mulch in spring before weed seeds sprout. To conserve moisture, make sure your mulch is in place before the soil begins to get dry during summer or other times of drought. In late fall or early winter, mulch the frozen soil around newly planted, tender, or shallow-rooted plants with straw or pine boughs to keep the soil safely frozen all winter.

The secret to making mulch most efficient is to apply a layer that is thick enough to block light and conserve moisture but not so thick as to pack down and become impenetrable.

MAXIMUM MULCH APPLICATION DEPTHS

MATERIAL	MAXIMUM DEPTH
Twice-shredded bark	1 inch
Coarse sand or shredded bark	2 inches
Cocoa-bean hulls	2 inches
Gravel	3 inches
Wood chips	3 to 4 inches
Bark nuggets	4 to 6 inches
Straw	6 to 8 inches

WISE WAYS
to WATER

There is nothing new about irrigation, which has been used since ancient Egyptian times, except the efficiency of modern methods. Egyptians dug gravity-fed dikes to water their gardens of tropical plants and exotic flowers. American pioneers pumped their irrigation water by hand from a well—a laborious way to tend their crops. In the 1950s, sprinklers were developed, making irrigation much more manageable and starting a trend toward dramatically increased water consumption.

The way that water flows freely from the tap and out into the garden gives the appearance that it is endless, which makes it easy for us to take water for granted and to carelessly overuse it. Because we can (and not necessarily because we should), gardeners have used irrigation to create green lawns and yards, so that even the desert can resemble the moist Midwest and East Coast.

Irrigation, which increases agricultural productivity, has become vital for feeding the growing world population. Irrigated feedstuff fields in the United States grew from 5 million acres in 1899 to more than 25 million acres in 1982. At the same time, use of groundwater for irrigation has grown from 20 billion gallons per day in 1950 to almost 50 billion gallons in 1985.

Water is also needed for washing and drinking, generating electricity, and manufacturing. Each 12-ounce soda can uses 66.6 quarts of water to make and deliver, and even more to fill. These kinds of water expenditures have more than doubled our daily water use —from 35 billion gallons of water per day in 1950 to almost 80 billion gallons per day in 1985.

This kind of growth cannot continue unabated. Water is a finite element; it's not created anew but instead shuttled between atmosphere and earth. As water use increases, there won't always be enough water to go around, a fact that people in arid western states have come to accept as a way of life. According to a University of Colorado study, water conservation is easily carried out in communities with watering restrictions or metered water payments. The big bill that comes with unlimited summer-lawn watering, car washing, and water play quickly teaches the economic repercussions of squandering water.

In many homes, fully half of all water used goes to the landscape. Learning to conserve water outdoors can make a significant impact. The gardener has the option of irrigating some instead

AVOIDING WASTEFUL WATERING

Several easy-to-follow guidelines will help you make the most of water in your garden.

- Avoid sprinkling in the middle of the day, particularly in hot weather.
- Don't water automatically. Instead irrigate only when natural rainfall is limited.
- Limit overhead sprinkling when brisk wind will send the water flying.
- In heavy soils, apply water in several watering sessions to encourage penetration instead of runoff.
- Water drought-tolerant plants less than those that love water.

of all of the yard or of growing plants able to tolerate a dry spell without pause. In regions where water is a precious commodity, many gardeners choose to grow plantings of locally adapted, drought-tolerant species, a technique called xeriscaping (see page 7).

Saving water in the landscape is not a black-or-white issue. There are many intermediate paths to take, ways to make water work harder and last longer, while still growing favorite plants and having a beautiful landscape. Knowing how to use water-efficient irrigation is as much art as it is science.

CHOOSING THE MOST EFFICIENT IRRIGATION SYSTEMS

Look to nature for clues about how best to water. A long, gentle rain that beats softly on an umbrella or patio overhang can moisten the ground and seep in deeply. In contrast, a thunderstorm with tree-shaking gusts of wind and white sheets of pelting rain hits the ground hard, compressing fine soils, bouncing and running off, and carrying away topsoil, nutrients, and organic matter.

It may seem fairly obvious that applying water gently is the best way to preserve healthy soil and, as a consequence, a healthy garden. Unfortunately, the overhead sprinklers whirring throughout the neighborhood on Saturday afternoons produce fat, hard-pounding water droplets similar to those of a thunderstorm. Gentle and highly efficient watering calls for more sophisticated drip and trickle irrigation systems, which apply a low volume of water at the soil surface.

Whichever method is chosen, homeowners can save water by irrigating garden areas, particularly those needing little water, separately from the thirsty lawn. Standard sprinklers, which are good for covering an expanse of ground, can manage the turf area while trickle irrigation works effectively in shrub and flower beds.

With the many kinds of irrigation equipment available today, it is easy to become overly ambitious, drowning landscapes with water under the pretense of providing tender, loving care. This is particularly true with automatic watering systems: How many times have you seen sprinklers spraying water regardless of the rain falling around them? The Denver Water Office of Water Conservation states that 85 percent of all landscape problems come from overwatering. As explained on page 39, soil saturation can be as hazardous to plants as drought. Adjusting the watering schedule to supplement nature, rather than

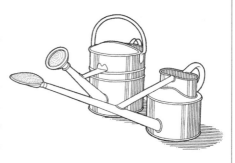

Old-fashioned watering can (left) and Haws watering can (right).

marching along regardless of the weather, is a first step toward water conservation and a healthy yard. "Don't water on automatic. Respond to your lawn's need, not your habit," suggests Denver Water in its brochure "Why the Grass Is Always Greener."

Another simple but often overlooked water-saving basic is to tweak watering frequencies to make sure that all the water applied will be absorbed into the soil. To do this, learn how much water the irrigation system applies in a given time period and how much moisture the soil can absorb, then synchronize the two in a harmonious give-and-take. Measure the amount of water delivered by overhead sprinklers by setting empty tuna fish or coffee cans or, better yet, Pyrex measuring cups around the lawn to capture water. Run the sprinkler for 15 minutes. Shut off the water and use a ruler to measure how much has collected in the container. From this amount, calculate how many inches, or fractions of an inch, will fall in an hour.

The next step is to determine the amount of water the soil can absorb. Run the sprinkler long enough to deliver an inch of water. If the water puddles or runs off, the soil cannot accept a full inch of moisture. Instead, try to provide the same inch of water in two half-hour sessions separated by an hour or two of breathing time.

A discussion of watering options, organized in order of increasing complexity and sophistication, follows.

USING WATERING CANS: An old-fashioned tin watering can, with a stubby-necked pouring spout and broad durable handle that arches over the filling well, has been used in homes and on farmsteads for decades. Gift stores now feature crafty versions of these enduring workhorses—hand-painted metal watering cans adorned with flowers, hummingbirds, and vines. They double as garden implements and decorations for a windowsill or front porch.

Often made of lightweight, durable polyethylene, contemporary watering cans have more innovative designs. While tin watering cans may be too tall to fill up in the kitchen sink, a squat, oval watering can is specifically made to fit under an ordinary

Double your load to double your efficiency.

faucet. This design also has an elevated filling hole that keeps water from splashing out when the watering can is full. Many watering cans have long, narrow watering spouts that are easy to work in and among crowded plants and deliver water to precisely the right spot. Most come with an oval, finely perforated watering rose that can be attached to the end of the spout to break up water into fine streams for smaller plants and seedlings.

Watering cans are integral parts of most people's first gardening experiences and, like a first love, remain near and dear to their hearts. Elementary school children growing peat pots of marigolds or snap beans, homemakers brightening their houses with tropical foliage or pots of bright azaleas (*Rhododendron* spp.) and daffodils

The classic watering can is indispensable even if you have a high-tech irrigation system.

(*Narcissus* spp.), and seniors collecting African violets (*Saintpaulia* spp.) or orchids all use watering cans to nourish and nurture their potted plants.

Watering cans personalize the act of watering. The gardener fills and carries the can, controlling the flow and the placement. Burrowing in amid the leaves to find the soil reveals the crown where the shoots emerge, new leaves, and other intimate elements of the plant. Watering becomes a time for inspection. Are the plants thriving, or do they need more light or humidity, a larger pot or fresh soil? Is that curled leaf still unraveling from the bud, or does

Watering by hand is time-consuming but provides a chance to inspect your garden closely.

it harbor aphids or mealybugs? Like preventative maintenance, these observations head off problems before they have a chance to get started.

But like any good thing, use of the watering can may be taken to extremes. The most common cause of potted plant failure is overwatering. Providing a drizzling every other day, whether a plant needs it or not, can swamp the potting soil and deprive the roots of air.

THE ART OF WATERING CONTAINER PLANTS: Container plants, especially those located indoors or under the front porch roof, rely exclusively on gardeners to keep them watered. Without rainfall to moisten pots occasionally, it is entirely up to the gardener to cater to their needs.

There are several ways to tell if a potted plant needs water: When container plants get thirsty, you will see color changes in potting soil and clay pots. Peat-based mixes turn from medium brown to light brown and clay pots become a lighter color than when wet. A parched peat-based potting mix will shrink away from the sides of the pot—and the plant itself will begin to wilt.

If you are unsure whether a container plant needs watering, you can perform these simple tests: If the pot is small or medium-sized, you can lift it up. A dry pot will feel much lighter than it does when you have just watered it. In addition, a finger stuck down into the potting soil will feel dry and have no residue. A pencil poked down into the soil will not emerge dark and wet. You can also buy water minders, gadgets which make it clear when the pot has dried out enough to warrant watering. Plant Pets, for instance, are ceramic probes shaped like animals that chirp or ribbit when the potting soil gets dry.

How you approach watering container pots will depend on what kind of condition the soil is in. If the soil is in firm contact with the sides of the pot, you can water from above. Fill the pot to the top rim with water, preferably lukewarm

WATERING ALTERNATIVES FOR POTTED PLANTS

People without the time or inclination to water potted plants regularly will be glad to know that hand-watering can be a thing of the past. Planting in self-watering pots or adding automatic watering systems to existing pots can take care of this job.

- Use self-watering pots with submerged sensors or wicks that siphon moisture up from an attached water reservoir when the soil gets dry.
- Water smaller pots from the bottom by resting them on a moist capillary mat made of water-absorbent fiber and connected to a reservoir.
- Devise an automatic watering system of drip irrigation–type tubes and drippers, which are available in prepackaged container garden watering kits.

for heat-loving tropical plants and summer flowers. You may need to refill large pots several times to moisten the soil thoroughly. When plenty of water emerges from bottom drainage holes, the soil is sufficiently wet. To prevent oversaturation, empty drainage water that collects in the pot saucer.

If the soil is very dry and has shriveled away from the pot sides, water applied from above will escape through the gaps between pot and potting soil, hardly moistening the soil at all. To avoid this problem, set the pot—plant and all—in a bucket partly filled with water, letting moisture soak in through the bottom drainage holes and the sides of a clay pot. Let the pot soak for a few minutes, until the soil feels moist at the surface and has become plump, filling out the entire pot. When you remove the pot from the bucket, let the excess water drain out freely.

The ability of a watering can to focus water on a precise, albeit small, site can be helpful when transplanting. Use a large watering can to fill each planting hole with water-soluble fertilizer solution before inserting a seedling. With quick access to water and nutrients, seedlings begin growing immediately, moving quickly on their way to getting established and gaining self-sufficiency.

A watering can is also useful for newly planted perennials in hard-to-reach places, for annuals brought into the garden in midseason for color, and for plants that need more water than their neighbors.

While the watering can is ideal for potted plants, its capabilities pale when it comes to watering gardens. The huge water-holding capacity of the soil quickly overwhelms the limited reserves in even the largest watering can, which will only moisten a meager area of dry soil.

DRAGGING A HOSE: Most outdoor planting projects usually require a hose, that ubiquitous green-, gray-, or rust-colored cylinder piled in a coil or left in a tangled heap in many yards. Hoses make household water available to all corners of the yard and can be used for washing cars and masonry as well as for watering. A stiff spray is often the best possible nonchemical control for aphids.

Hoses are such basics that they are often taken for granted, whether left lying along the path in an elegant garden or snaked beside the foundation planting ready for use. When they are tidied up and put away the yard looks much less cluttered, but hose dragging is hard work. After pulling the hose into place, many gardeners find it easier to leave it there, ready for action.

An outstretched hose may not be safe, however. If pulled across a front walk, it may trip a package-burdened deliveryman or a friendly neighbor. A green hose that's been abandoned on the lawn may blend into the background, only to be run over by an adolescent with a mower.

Garden accessories are beginning to render hose dragging obsolete. Hose caddies and carriers—rotating reels set on wheels to pull through the yard—make hoses almost as easy to put away in the garage or garden shed as a hoe and shovel. Two- and four-wheeled designs are available; the latter offer stability and ease of handling but command a higher price. Steel-frame caddies are made for lifetime duty. Less expensive plastic versions may last only a season or two with heavy use. Alternatively, hose reels or simple hose hooks made of basic plastic or sculpted metal can be stationed in the garden to cut down on dragging.

While all hoses will transport water, not all perform equally well. The more expensive of the lot, multilayered five-ply hoses made of rubber or polyester cords, are custom-designed to remain limber without kinking, splitting, or stiffening as inexpensive plastic kinds do. They earn their purchase price in long life and convenience. Some can be guaranteed for a decade, but you need to keep receipts and warranty information on file to cash in on a hose that proves to be a lemon in five to seven years.

Even with the best hose, an attempt to hand-water an entire garden, particularly a very dry garden, will prove successful for only a dedicated individual willing to keep at it for a very long time. A light 15-minute squirt may dampen only the top inch of earth. It is unlikely to provide the deep drenching that helps mature plants. For prolonged watering, sprinklers, soaker hoses, or irrigation systems, which never run out of patience are better choices (see pages 81, 89, and 95).

Watering with a hand-held hose can be a source of soil trauma, as the downpour may hit the surface hard enough to bounce

A spray lance, or Water Wand, is useful for watering seeds and flower beds and can provide a gentle mist or a soaking stream.

seeds and young seedlings right out of the ground. Attempting to soften the impact by holding your finger over the spout may freeze the digit long before the job is complete. A more suitable way to break up heavy flow is by fitting the hose with a water-propelling mist nozzle or a water breaker that separates the flow into tiny streams.

Among the handiest water breakers are Water Wands, which have a head similar to a watering can rose on a long handle that lets you deliver water anywhere you want it. It's ideal for watering hanging baskets, without having to pull them down or climb up on a stepladder. You can find Water Wands of varying lengths for large gardens, patios, and pots. A bubbler, another form of water breaker, is a cylindrical device full of holes (and remarkably similar to a tea ball) that you can screw on the end of the hose. A fan head, which is triangular and perforated with holes on the broad end, sometimes comes with a leg that will prop the spout up. You can leave it in the garden to soak a large clump of Siberian irises (*Iris sibirica*), a newly planted hydrangea (*Hydrangea* spp.), or other plants in the immediate vicinity.

Hose-end spraying nozzles are ideal for the gardener who prefers to stand in one place and shoot the water out to where it is needed. Some spraying nozzles are all-purpose and others are designed specifically for the garden. Among the best are twisting brass nozzles, which are simple, effective, and inexpensive. They can be adjusted to provide a fine mist spray for watering seed beds, a cone of medium sized droplets for watering trees and shrubs, or a narrow jet stream for knocking mud off the tires of your car.

Pistol-grip-type nozzles, which are common, require steady pressure on the trigger to emit water. Unfortunately, your hand is likely to tire before a big watering job is completed. If you like this kind of nozzle, look for ergonomically effective alternatives that are easy on your hands. The MultiFlow Nozzle, for instance, has a lightweight plastic spray head, angled to allow it to penetrate between plants without twisting your wrist, and a large, easy-to-hold grip. A sliding thumb valve allows you to adjust the spray from mist, to cone, or jet.

When pulling a hose taut to spray a distant corner of the garden, you will quickly learn another, less desirable trait of the garden hose. It will stretch across the garden bed, crushing peppers, flowers, basil, and other plants in its way. This shouldn't come as a surprise, since the shortest path between two points is a straight line. Still, even experienced gardeners focused on reaching a last, distant corner of the yard, succumb to the urge to tug on the hose and, in doing so, pull it into forbidden garden territory.

A discerning gardener will plan ahead to protect the garden from pushy hoses by putting hose guides in the corners, at ends of rows, or around the perimeter of the garden. Hose guides can be any kind of upright sentinel that will hold a hose back. Wooden stakes, vertical rocks, and elegant commercial pillars of terra-cotta or metal will all serve this purpose. Make sure the hose guide you choose is anchored well enough so it won't be bowled over by the hose and tall enough so that a flexing coil can't jump over it.

SPRINKLERS: A natural companion for a hose is a sprinkler, a device designed to send water shooting across wide open spaces. A sprinkler is lightweight; you can readily move it around the yard, and easily monitor it by looking out the window. It may attract hovering hummingbirds who shower in the glittering droplets.

Sprinklers are anything but efficient, however. On a hot or windy day, much of the water evaporates before it hits the ground. What water does fall indiscriminately moistens weeds, walks, drives, siding, and other structures that don't need watering—sometimes only a small percentage soaks the soil around thirsty cultivated plants. Droplets fall hard and fast, pummeling the soil. They moisten foliage and can encourage leaf spots and other diseases on susceptible plants like roses (*Rosa* spp.), delphiniums (*Delphinium* spp.), phlox (*Phlox* spp.), and speedwell (*Veronica* spp.).

Despite the disadvantages of sprinklers, they have a part to play in the garden, so it's smart to shop for the most efficient and effective model. You

CATCH PESTS COLD

A cold blast of water from the hose, particularly when you don't expect it, can take your breath away. Water DeFence is a new product that uses this startle factor to keep wildlife and unwanted pests out of your garden. An infrared heat and motion sensor tracks the approach of unwanted visitors such as deer, raccoons, birds, and dogs, and sprays them with a 3- to 4-second blast of water. Water DeFence has a sprinkler head mounted on a 17-inch-high post and is powered by a 9-volt battery. It sells for more than $100.

A SEASONAL GUIDE TO WATERING AND WATER CONSERVATION

Use this general guide to plan a water-wise strategy for your landscape. Keep in mind, however, that you will need to alter the scheme according to the weather and the kinds of plants you are growing. The four seasons below are based not on the calendar year but on changes in weather that alter garden conditions.

FALL SEASON

Cool Climate
- Water evergreens during dry weather.
- Continue to water late-summer plantings and any other new nursery stock.
- Plant hardy bulbs, which probably won't need any extra watering.
- Plant hardy annuals such as pansies and China pinks for flowers now and in spring.
- Plant large balled-and-burlapped or container-grown nursery stock, making a watering saucer beneath each plant.
- Shred fallen leaves and till them into the soil of annual or vegetable gardens.
- Start a compost pile with fallen autumn leaves, seed-free weeds, and disease- and pest-free stems from garden cleanup.
- Coil up your garden hoses and soaker hoses and put them in the garage for safe storage.
- Flush out drip irrigation lines now and again before spring arrives so they'll be ready to use.

Warm Climate
- Plant balled-and-burlapped or container-grown perennials and nursery stock.
- Plant hardy annuals such as pansies and China pinks for flowers now and in spring.
- Water evergreens during dry weather.
- Continue to water new plantings from this or the previous year.
- Plant hardy bulbs, which won't need any extra watering.
- Shred fallen leaves and till them into the soil of annual or vegetable gardens.
- Start a compost pile with seed-free weeds, disease- and pest-free stems from garden cleanup, and autumn leaves.

Hot Climate
- Add abundant organic matter to the soil to keep it moisture retentive.
- Organic matter decomposes rapidly in your climate. Continue making your own compost from seed-free weeds and disease- and pest-free stems from garden cleanup.
- Plant flowers, herbs, and vegeta-

bles that make the most of the more moderate winter weather.

- Plant nursery stock, making a watering basin below each tree

and shrub and installing drip irrigation if you live in a dry climate.

- Mulch the garden to help keep the soil cool and moist.

WINTER SEASON

Cool Climate

- Snow cover can insulate plant roots and provide moisture for the soil when it melts.
- Avoid using salt on icy areas because salt can contaminate the soil. Substitute garden-safe icebreakers.
- Use the off-season to plan your xeriscaping or drip irrigation system.
- Browse through nursery catalogs for drought-tolerant plants.
- Mulch shallow-rooted plants, evergreens like lavender that are prone to winter burn, or new plantings with an airy mulch such as pine boughs or straw once the soil is solidly frozen. Plan to remove the mulch before plants break dormancy in spring. Avoid winter mulches where soils are heavy—a mulch will make them even soggier.

Warm Climate

- Hardy plants survive soggy winter weather best in well-drained soils. Evaluate whether you have garden areas that need improved drainage.
- Avoid using salt on icy areas near

the garden because salt can contaminate the soil. Substitute garden-safe icebreakers.

- Mulch shallow-rooted plants, evergreens like lavender that are prone to winter burn, or new plantings with an airy mulch such as pine boughs or straw once the soil is solidly frozen. Plan to remove the mulch before plants break dormancy in spring. Avoid winter mulches where soils are heavy—a mulch will make them even soggier.
- You may be able to continue planting container-grown nursery stock. Make a watering basin below each tree and shrub.

Hot Climate

- Plant and water as needed. When planting nursery stock, make a watering basin below each tree and shrub and install drip irrigation if you live in a dry climate.
- Continue to add organic matter to the soil and to mulch for water conservation.
- Browse through nursery catalogs for drought-tolerant plants.

SPRING SEASON

Cool Climate

- Sow lawn grass seeds, mulch them with straw, and water regularly

until well established.

- After the last spring frost, plant sod and keep it well watered.

- Plant bare-root roses, perennials, and strawberries. If these arrive too early, when the soil is still too soggy to work, you can pot them in large containers for transplanting later.
- Add extra compost and other organic material to the soil, tilling it in or laying it on top.
- Plant cool-season vegetables and flowers. If rains are regular, they may not need much additional watering.
- Plant perennials, shrubs, and trees, making watering saucers beneath each one.
- Install drip irrigation or soaker hoses in perennial beds before the foliage fills in. You may not have to use them until summer.
- Remove winter mulches as soon as the weather breaks. Once the soil has changed from soggy to nicely moist, mulch to conserve moisture. Watch out for slugs that can thrive in cool mulch at this time of the season.

Warm Climate

- Plant early. Use heat-tolerant species for later plantings.
- Sow lawn grass seeds or plugs,

mulch with straw, and water regularly until well established.
- Plant bare-root roses, perennials, and strawberries. Soak the roots in a wet mud slurry 8 hours before planting. Provide plenty of water until the plants are growing strongly.
- Mulch beds and borders to help keep roots cool.
- Plant flowers in containers with water reservoirs at the bottom to keep the soil moist longer.

Hot Climate

- As the weather heats up, plant water needs will increase. Get a good sprinkler and look into using soaker hoses or drip irrigation.
- Start early if you want to plant nursery stock so it can be established before the arrival of summer heat. Make a watering saucer below each plant and keep them all moist.
- Continue to add mulch and organic matter to the garden.
- Plant most warm-season grass seeds or plugs in early spring, mulch with straw, and water regularly until well established.

SUMMER SEASON

Cool Climate

- Plant warm season vegetables and flowers including summer-flowering bulbs. Water regularly until they are well established. Drought-tolerant species can make do with less after

growing strongly.
- Keep potted plants moist, which may mean daily watering when the weather is hot.
- When the weather is hot and dry, you will have to water regularly.

It's still not too late to add a soaker hose or drip irrigation system to the property.

- When the weather becomes dry, make a list of the drought-tolerant plants that grow well with little irrigation. You may want to plant more of them in the fall.
- If you have not mulched gardens already, you can do so now.
- It is possible to plant container-grown plants in early or midsummer, but expect to water them lavishly if you don't want to lose them in the heat. The cooling temperatures of late summer make it a good time for planting, second only to spring. You can sow lawn grasses and plant a variety of container-grown or balled-and-burlapped nursery stock.
- In midsummer, you can replant cool-season vegetables and flowers, but they will need regular watering and perhaps also afternoon shade to get established.
- Catch extra water in a rain barrel or harvest gray water for the garden.
- Plant flowers in containers with water reservoirs at the bottom to keep the soil moist longer.

Warm Climate
- When the weather is hot and dry, you will have to water regularly. It's not too late to add a soaker hose or drip irrigation system to the yard.

- If you have not mulched gardens already, you can do so now.
- Provide light afternoon shade to plants that don't tolerate heat well.
- When the weather becomes dry, make a list of the drought-tolerant plants that grow well with little irrigation. You may want to plant more of them in the fall.
- It is possible to plant container-grown plants, but expect to water them lavishly if you don't want to lose them in the heat.
- Catch extra water in a rain barrel or harvest gray water for the garden (see pages 99–100).

Hot Climate
- Blazing temperatures make this your down season. Use it to plan new xeriscaping and drip irrigation systems.
- Continue to water to support the existing landscape during dry weather.
- Provide light afternoon shade to plants that don't tolerate heat well.
- Continue to add organic matter and mulch to garden beds.
- When the weather becomes dry, make a list of the drought-tolerant plants that grow well with little irrigation. You may want to plant more of them in the fall.
- Catch extra water in a rain barrel or harvest gray water for the garden.

will find many of the newest sprinklers are partly composed of rugged plastic, which has its own good and bad points. Although durable and lightweight, plastic is more likely to flip over than heavier metal sprinklers.

For a long life, look for a sprinkler with a top-quality coupler, the crucial fitting that attaches the hose to the sprinkler. The coupler should be deep, easy to turn, and designed with a washer that won't pop out and allow the connection to leak.

Make sure the model you choose can be adjusted to apply more or less water to smaller or larger spaces. Adjustments should be easy to make, without having to dig a how-to manual out of the filing cabinet, so it is convenient to vary sprinkler patterns as needed.

How effective an overhead sprinkler will be depends mostly on the kind of sprinkler you use and the size and water needs of the plants you have. You can select from sprinklers that oscillate, circle, or bubble up in one place.

Oscillating Sprinklers. This classic design features a rectangular body and long, narrow cylindrical head covered with small pores that break up water as it emerges. The head rotates back and forth, sending an arching spray of water high into the air. One advantage of high-flying water delivery is that it is less prone to being blocked by larger plants, making it work as well in a flower garden as in the lawn.

PLANNING THE VEGETABLE GARDEN FOR EFFICIENT SPRINKLER WATERING

Before planting your vegetable garden, consider where you want to put the sprinkler and situate the crops to allow equal access to the water.

If your vegetable garden is divided by a central path, you can put the sprinkler in the middle of the garden. Plant low-growing crops such as bush beans, carrots, and lettuce toward the center, because they won't block the spray, and put taller crops such as caged tomatoes and sunflowers around the perimeter.

For a garden without a central-access path, you may have to put the sprinkler at the perimeter of the garden, directing the spray toward the interior. In this situation, you should plant lower crops around the garden edge and taller crops toward the inside.

Airborne moisture is easily windblown, however, and even a gentle breeze can shift it away from the intended garden target. Because the small pores in the sprinkler head can become blocked, look for models you can take apart and clean if necessary.

Many models of oscillating sprinklers are easy to adjust, so you can fine-tune their delivery area and flow rate. There are four watering patterns to select from—a full cycle in which the head turns from left to right and back for watering from the center of a garden; a half-cycle in either direction for watering from the edge of a garden or lawn; and a motionless fully upright spray for small areas.

Water is not always applied evenly by oscillating sprinklers; some models hesitate and release extra water before rotating back in a new direction. To check how evenly water is distributed, set empty soup cans a foot apart in a line that cuts across the area being watered. Turn on the sprinkler for a half hour and then compare how much water has accumulated in each can. If some cans are filled more fully than others, you will have to move the sprinkler more often to encourage even moisture levels throughout the garden.

Occasionally oscillating sprinklers can get stuck and won't rotate to complete the entire cycle, dumping their entire water load on a single area. It's a good idea to watch the sprinkler when it first starts out to make sure it is working properly before leaving it to do its job.

If you are willing to spend a little extra, you can find labor-saving oscillating sprinklers with timers that automatically turn them off. For watering among taller plants, look for a tripod-mounted sprinkler that can send its spray over the leafy canopies of shrubs and flowers.

It can be hard to tell which of the dozens of oscillating sprinklers available is the best. Perhaps this recommendation will help. A 1998 sprinkler trial conducted by the National Gardening Association found the Naan Whisper Quiet Oscillator (model 520) to be superior among a large field of oscillating sprinklers. It delivers water in a spray or mist in an easily adjusted watering pattern.

Circling Sprinklers. With two or three spinning arms that emit water at the ends, these sprinklers spray water more horizontally than vertically, minimizing evaporation and wind influence. They can be adjusted to water a full circle or as little as 15 percent of a circle. Look for a circling sprinkler with a stable base—a metal stand or deep soil-penetrating stake, for instance—which will help to keep the sprinkler from tipping over as its arms rotate. Because many can cover a 100-foot-wide circle (although water falls most heavily closer to the sprinkler), circling sprinklers work well in a large lawn or among expanses of low plants like ground covers. To use these sprinklers to water larger plants, find a model that can be mounted on top of a long-legged tripod.

The motion of the water-emitting arms is driven by one of two different mechanisms. Rotary systems use silent water-driven internal gears to twirl. They will let you hear the trills of birds and rustling of leaves as you water. Impulse sprinklers, in noisy contrast, use springs that make rhythmic chirps as the arms spin.

In National Gardening Association trials, the Melnor Rotary Lawn Sprinkler (model 2900) proved the best in the field. It has a stable sled-like base, quiet action, a choice of mist, medium, or large spray, and capacity to deliver water from 10 to 40 feet away.

Fixed-Spray Sprinklers. These simple sprinklers, used for watering low-growing plants in a small space, allow water to push up and out of one or multiple holes like a miniature geyser. Like a bubbling hose nozzle, a fixed-spray sprinkler delivers water under its own power so it does not shoot for any distance. Some models look like perforated doughnuts while others are crafted to resemble frogs. Choose a fixed-spray sprinkler that is heavy enough so it won't flip over, a common problem with this type. The National Gardening Association preferred the Melnor 4-Way Tureet (model 675). It has changeable nozzles that let it cover a variety of watering patterns—square, rectangular, and narrow or wide strips.

Other Sprinklers. Sculpturelike sprinklers of copper tubing shaped into outlines of butterflies, swans, or other graceful creatures are one of the newest developments. As they spin they make rainbows of droplets when the sun hits the water just right. What they lose in efficiency, they make up for in beauty. However, these sprinklers are more expensive.

If you get tired of moving your sprinkler around the yard (and if you are fond of gadgets), consider buying a walking sprinkler. The Rain Train has a motor that pushes it along the hose, spinning and spraying an expanse of lawn all by itself. It can apply water on light, medium, or heavy cycles and in sprays reaching 15, 35, or 50 feet away.

You can also find a watering system and weed barrier all in one in a new product called Water's Edge. The weed barrier is a 6½-inch-wide plastic strip pressed down into the soil to prevent roots of grass or weeds from working into the garden. At the top is a water line dotted with regularly spaced sprinkler outlets that come to life when connected to a garden hose. Because a 10-foot-long strip costs more than $30, this is not a good choice for a budget-minded gardener.

In climates with abundant rainfall and water for irrigation, overhead sprinklers will be used in many landscapes. Where water is in short supply, however, soaker hoses and drip irrigation will help make a little water go a long way.

SOAKER HOSES: The biggest change in watering technology has come from the revelation that water need not be flung through the air like rain. Instead, it can trickle gently into the earth from ground level like an artesian spring. This eliminates most of the problems of evaporation and soil compaction caused by overhead watering. It also limits foliage wetting and the resulting spread of diseases.

It may take some time for a gardener used to the splash and flamboyance of sprinkling to adapt to ground-level watering. Because the action is low, it's hard to tell how much moisture has been delivered without digging in for a closer look. Let the soaker hose run for an hour or more, then dig a hole nearby to see if it has moistened the soil at least a foot deep, the minimum needed for most mature plants. It also helps to watch the surface of the earth for runoff, which is proof that the soil can hold no more moisture. Just as with call-waiting, e-mail, and VCRs, spending a little time to learn how to use ground-level irrigation can save effort in the long run.

One way to experiment with ground-level watering is with inexpensive soaker hoses made of water-seeping canvas or permeable rubber from recycled tires. Soaker hoses are designed to be moved through the garden, although some rubber models can be buried under a few inches of mulch or soil and kept semipermanently in place. Inexpensive canvas

INSTALLING A SOAKER HOSE

Soaker hoses are easy to install and use. They work best on level ground, but even then are likely to release more moisture near where they attach to the hose.

1. Install the soaker hose while plants are small, so you can work it among them without damaging foliage and branches. In a perennial bed, install the hose in spring so it will be ready to use especially during droughts.

2. Unwind the hose and gently run it between plants or, better yet, run it straight through the bed. Put the hose close enough to plants to thoroughly moisten their roots. But don't let it rest on or touch emerging herbaceous stems. This portion of the plant, called the crown, is susceptible to rotting if kept too wet.

3. Leave the coupling end of the soaker hose at the edge of the bed, in a location where it is easy for you to hook it up to the garden hose.

4. Connect the garden hose to the soaker hose and turn on the water to take a trial run. Make sure the hose is not kinked and that water emerges from the entire length of the hose.

5. Allow the soaker hose to work for an hour, then turn it off. Dig down in the soil to see how far the water has spread so you can determine if you have watered long enough. Consider whether you need to add another soaker hose or two to cover all the soil that needs watering.

6. If you buy a soaker hose that can be put semi-permanently in place, cover it with bark mulch or hay.

hoses need to be coiled and stored in a dry place after each use to keep them from rotting.

Soaker hoses can be laid in straight lines down the rows of a vegetable or cutting garden or gently woven between clusters of perennials or shrubs. Avoid sharp turns, which can make the hoses kink and cut off the water supply. Expect to see more water delivered at the top of the hose, near where it connects to the water source, and less at the bottom. Inconsistent water delivery is one of the biggest problems with soaker hoses, although some designs claim to have overcome it. Most rubber soaker hoses perform best if connected to a fine filter to prevent particulates in tap water from clogging up the weeping pores.

How many soaker hoses are needed to irrigate a garden depends on soil type. In sandy soil, where moisture moves downward instead of laterally, hoses should be spaced closer together than in denser soils. When used in a vegetable garden, where only planting rows need moistening and paths or open spaces surrounding them can be kept dry, put one soaker hose along each row.

COMPARING SOAKER HOSES AND DRIP IRRIGATION

While both soaker hoses and drip irrigation deliver water slowly at ground level, they are different. Soaker hoses are inexpensive and suitable for moving around the garden. Drip irrigation is a more permanent arrangement, custom-designed for the needs of your garden plants.

TYPE	SOAKER HOSES	DRIP IRRIGATION
Ground-level watering	yes	yes
Overhead watering	no	yes, with microsprinklers and sprayers
Low-volume water application	yes	yes
Expense	low	moderate to high
Even application rate	no, flow heavier near origin of water	yes, with pressure-compensating emitters
Increased flow for special needs	no	yes
Preplanning required	no	yes
Design flexibility	best in straight lines or gentle curves	very flexible

New twists on the old soaker hose design have been created to meet the needs of special plants around the landscape. For instance, watering tubes are available to encircle the base of a newly planted tree or shrub and seep water down over the root ball for several days to encourage root establishment and growth. Such novelties may cost as much as a one-month water bill and may not actually prove more efficient than letting a hose trickle over the root ball. But if they ensure that the job gets done, they will guarantee the future of a valuable tree.

FLOOD IRRIGATION OF SUNKEN BEDS: While in moist climates beds may be raised to encourage good drainage in wet weather, in dry climates you may want to sink garden beds or planting areas to collect and concentrate limited rain or irrigation water.

Vegetable Gardening in Trenches. Some of the best arid climate vegetable gardens are grown in sunken trenches; the earthen walls help to shade the soil, reduce evaporation, and cool moisture-loving tomatoes, peppers, and lettuce.

Where rain seldom falls or a drought becomes prolonged, trenches can be 6 inches deep without fear they will collapse in a downpour. Where rain does occasionally occur or topsoil is shallow, make trenches only about 3 inches deep. If the soil washes down on the roots of tomatoes, they will thrive, rooting all along the soil-covered stem. Moisture-hungry potatoes, too, are ideal for shallow trenches, producing more tubers in soil that accumulates around the submerged stem.

When trench-grown vegetables need water, you can run a soaker hose through a long trench or let a hose trickle into a short trench, both methods ensuring the water reaches thirsty roots. Let irrigation water run until the soil is deeply moistened, simulating rainfall of 1 to 2 inches a week. Thorough watering is particularly important in arid climates, where you need to wash excess salts out of the soil to prevent damage to plant roots.

Watering Saucers. In both arid and drought-prone regions, more decorative ornamental beds of well-drained soil can be made in a slightly dished fashion, giving the landscape more shape and interest while capturing water for the plants within. This is particularly effective beneath newly planted trees and shrubs (see page 50) that need to be kept moist until well established. You can flood soil depressions with a garden hose or using a hose connected to the roof downspout to direct water to where it is needed most.

To deeply moisten good gar-den loam to 6 feet deep below a 6-inch-deep watering basin, let a hose trickle into the basin until it is full. After the water drains down, fill it up again. Sandy soil may need only one filling to do the same job, but you will have to

A bed dug below soil level remains cooler than the surrounding soil, and the basin shape helps to retain moisture.

water it more frequently to keep the area evenly moist. Clay soil, in which water moves slowly, may need to be refilled four times to be deeply moistened but will hold that moisture for a week or more.

In regions with regular rain, these trenches can be counterproduc-tive, however. If the soil is not well drained or rainfall is abundant, plants can sit and rot in water. The exceptions to this rule are bog plants like Japanese and Louisiana irises (*Iris* spp.) and water cannas (*Canna* hyb.), which will thrive in constantly moist, plastic-lined trenches.

CUSTOMIZED WATERING SYSTEMS: Sprinklers and soaker hoses are off-the-rack country cousins to highly efficient and personally tailored irrigation systems. Sprinklers and soaker hoses perform similarly any-where in the nation, requiring the gardener to make adjustments in spac-ing and watering duration to fit the soil and adjust for rainfall differences.

Customized systems, in contrast, are specially designed to provide ideal coverage for a single yard—not the neighbor's yard or that of a gar-dener in another state. Getting the setup right takes considerable initial effort, but once installed a watering system can be easy to handle and effective. While it is possible to plan a customized system, all but the most experienced do-it-yourselfer would be well advised to consult a professional to make sure this vital step is implemented correctly. The effort can offer rewards in years to come with a thriving landscape, sav-ings on water bills, and no further need to drag hoses around.

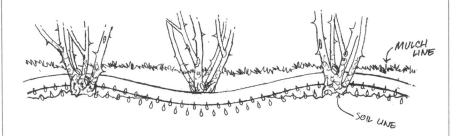

Drip irrigation can be customized to provide an ideal amount of water to specific plants.

An in-ground irrigation system can be as permanent as driveways and walks. It is installed underground, where it works unseen and is safe from mowers and the deteriorating effects of ultraviolet rays on plastics. It can be used with traditional sprinklers and drip irrigation, or a combination of the two.

In-ground plumbing, as the name implies, is unobtrusively installed below the soil surface. Because installation involves digging and disruption, it is best done before landscaping or at the start of a landscape renovation project.

System design is the most vital element of an in-ground irrigation system. It must be adapted to the existing plumbing, rate of water flow, and water pressure. A backflow preventer will be required to ensure that irrigation water does not contaminate household water supplies. A pressure regulator can reduce the amount of water pressure to levels appropriate for the irrigation system; this step is particularly important for drip irrigation.

Irrigation systems may have a clocklike brain called a controller unit that governs when they turn on and off. The controller unit can be located on the back porch or in the garage or basement, anywhere it can be easily adjusted according to the season or month, amount of natural rainfall, and temperature. The best model for a water-efficient yard will allow separate scheduling of garden beds and lawn and use of short, repeating watering cycles needed to moisten heavy soils. Some systems add a rainfall sensor to prevent needless watering after rain.

Pipes will extend out into the yard, supplying water to sprinkler heads or drip irrigation tubes. A main line connected to household plumbing may be intercepted with zone valves, which open to provide water to lateral lines and sprinkler heads. Zone valves are needed to set different watering schedules for low-, moderate-, and high-water-use areas of the landscape.

Choose from a variety of sprinkler heads for lawn areas. Pop-up types emerge several inches above the lawn surface, arising like mushrooms on demand. They provide water in a circular pattern and can be adjusted for quarter-, half-, or full-circle water delivery. Rotor heads rotate and spray water; they have a longer reach and work well in larger yards. Similar action comes from gear-driven heads, which have a shorter reach and quieter action. For low-volume irrigation, microsprinklers and microsprayers provide fine sprays of water useful for beds of ground cover or low-growing flowers.

DRIP IRRIGATION: Drip irrigation—feeder lines and tubes resting on the soil surface or buried an inch or two deep in mulch or soil—can be attached to in-ground plumbing or a garden hose. Drip irrigation can be installed around existing plants and customized to provide an ideal amount of water. Unlike underground piping, drip lines are soft plastic and can be damaged by a sharp hoe or shovel as well as the nibblings of rodents.

Drip irrigation tubes allow water to seep from a perforated tube similar to a soaker hose or from emitter lines, tubes that release water to the plants from either multiple pores or special valves or mininozzles. These pores and emitters release predetermined

DRIP IRRIGATION STUDIES

Drip irrigation is proving its value in study after study, with benefits that apply to both home gardens and commercial agriculture. Cotton grown with subsurface drip irrigation had yields equal to or better than cotton grown with conventional irrigation systems and only used half the amount of water. In the alkaline soils of Egypt, cucumbers grown with drip irrigation under plastic mulch and field-grown tomatoes with subsurface drip irrigation suffered less from salt accumulation and had denser roots and higher yields than those grown using overhead watering.

amounts of water to nearby plants. To keep pores and emitters from clogging up with sediment or organic matter, filter tap water before it enters the drip lines. Clean the filters once a month during the growing season. Flush the system occasionally to help keep the irrigation tubes and emitters from clogging up. You can add a water-soluble fertilizer applicator to the system, but it increases clogging problems.

Drip irrigation is not spread uniformly over the entire garden; instead, it is applied to specific areas and allowed to spread through the soil. It is vital to plan the placement of lines and emitters to successfully moisten the entire root system of each plant on all sides and throughout its depth. Examples below illustrate some of the design variables:

• Smaller plants that have small, shallow root systems, such as tomato seedlings or lettuce, will need lighter and more frequent irrigation with closer-spaced emitters than deeper-rooted tomato plants or peonies.

• In sandy soils, water will penetrate more deeply with less lateral spread, requiring more closely spaced lines and emitters. With a flow rate of 1 gallon per hour, lines can be spaced as close as 1 to 2 feet apart to uniformly wet the soil.

• In loam soil, water spreads relatively evenly to make a rounded moistened area. With a flow rate of 1 gallon or slightly less per hour, lines can be spaced 2 to 2½ feet apart.

• In clay, the absorption and spread of irrigation water is limited and often creeps horizontally near the surface with little deep penetration. Using a low volume of water, 0.6 gallons per hour, lines can be spaced 2 to 3 feet apart.

A vegetable garden is a good place to experiment with do-it-yourself drip irrigation system design. Run a drip line down each row and send individual emitter lines to separate large plants like hills of squash or blueberry bushes. Another place to use drip irrigation is under plastic mulch; keep the water lines at least 6 inches away from the planting rows so they won't be damaged during planting.

If the garden plan changes or a better irrigation layout comes to mind, it's easy to switch the drip irrigation arrangement around. New connectors can be purchased separately and small plugs can fill holes left by unwanted drippers.

INSTALLING DRIP IRRIGATION IN A VEGETABLE GARDEN

Drip irrigation, with lines run straight down rows in a vegetable garden, is effective and easy to install. You can plan your own system or buy prepackaged vegetable garden irrigation kits. Always follow the manufacturer's instructions. General guidelines are:

1. Make a scale plan of the vegetable garden or bed you want to irrigate and sketch in rows.

2. Based on the garden plan, calculate the number of emitter lines necessary. You can run a single emitter line down 1- to 2-foot-wide beds that are going to be filled with carrots, beets, or lettuce, for example. You might also use a single emitter line between a closely spaced double row of beans. For more widely spaced rows of tomatoes or cucumbers, use one emitter line per row of plants. You'll have to alter these spacing recommendations as needed to accommodate specific soil types.

3. Install a pressure regulator on the trickle system to reduce water pressure coming out of the house to levels appropriate for the kind of trickle-irrigation system you are using. Add a fine filter screen to remove any clogging particles, and you should also put a back-flow preventer on the outdoor faucet to keep irrigation water separate from household water.

4. Install a main water line, perhaps of ½-inch-diameter polytubing, which will run down the side of the garden bed and connect to the garden hose or faucet and also to each emitter line.

5. Cut the emitter lines to the length of the rows and attach to the main line. Connect to the water source and flush any dirt out of the lines.

6. Insert the emitters that will work best in your soil into the lines as needed. A general rule is to place them every 12 inches in closely planted areas or use polytubing with preinstalled emitters. You can also put a single emitter at the base of more widely spaced plants. In dry climates, you could increase this to two emitters per mound of water-hungry plants like cucumbers.

7. Run the irrigation system, checking that all emitters are operational.

8. When the soil is dry, run the system for a half hour. Then turn it off and dig down to see how far the water has spread. Adjust the amount of time you water, and perhaps the position and type of emitters, accordingly.

Recycling Leftover Household Water and Rain

Pristine, drinking-quality water need not be the only choice for irrigating gardens, as murky swamps full of cattails (*Typha* spp.), rushes (*Juncus* spp.), and bald cypress (*Taxodium distichum*) can attest. Where tap water is scarce, diverted rainwater and household wash water can be used in its place.

USING RAINWATER: Many nurseries irrigate their crops with water pumped from holding ponds that is ripe with algae and other organics. Experienced gardeners, however, may prefer to water their potted plants with rainwater, an almost pure fluid free from chlorine, fluorine, and water softening salt that may be in tap water.

To collect rainfall, put a rain barrel, 5-gallon bucket, or even a large bowl in a convenient outdoor place—on the patio or beside the back door, for instance. Where space is limited, look for specially designed rain collectors with convenient options such as a flat, wall-hugging side and roof downspout hookup. A removable top prevents accumulation of insects and debris and a bottom tap makes filling watering cans easy.

Another option is to direct downspouts to spew water out into the garden. Attach a polyvinyl chloride elbow to the base of a downspout and use a flexible pipe to carry rainwater into the garden. This works particularly well in dished landscapes or sunken beds that allow irrigation water to collect and percolate down into areas needing it most.

Another way to make use of storm water is available to gardeners resurfacing their asphalt driveways. Build the pavement up near the house, creating a slight slope leading toward the yard. This will direct rainwater away from the foundation, which helps to keep the basement dry and the lawn moist.

Except for the occasional enormous rain that brings rivers up over their banks and turns parking lots into ponds, storm sewers need not be overflowing. With some creative thinking, previously wasted rainwater can be put to good use in the yard.

USING GRAY WATER: In the 4th century B.C., Aristotle noted that mankind consists of two kinds of people: those who are as thrifty as if they expect to live forever, and those who are as extravagant as if this was their last day on Earth. Environmentally conscious gardeners, who realize they are only borrowing the bountiful elements of nature, will likely be in the first group as will be those who have felt the pinch of water shortages. They may find ways to make the most of water, in whatever form it is found. In homes with softened water unacceptable for use on houseplants, for instance, the unwanted remainder of a half-drunk glass of bottled water will be poured on a nearby philodendron (*Philodendron* spp.) or umbrella tree (*Schefflera* spp.). Recycling household water in the garden works on the same principle, only on a much larger scale.

Saved from running into the sewer or septic system after showering or rinsing laundry, water can be funneled through special plumbing out into the yard. An average house can yield 100 gallons of this kind of gray water

HARVESTING GRAY WATER

Large-scale use of gray water will call for installing special plumbing and irrigation systems (see page 100). It's surprisingly easy, however, to collect gray water on a small scale. Keep an open mind and you will discover abundant opportunities, such as the following:

- Gather extra water with a bucket set in the corner of the shower.
- Empty day-old water from a pet bowl, tea kettle, or drinking glasses into a watering can.
- Put water changes from the goldfish bowl on heavy-feeding flowers in the garden.

- Cool water left after boiling vegetables, eggs, and pasta and pour it on the garden.
- Rinse hand-washed delicate fabrics over a tub to save the water.
- Rinse off your dirty or sandy feet in a large bucket and use that water on potted plants.
- Empty water from a children's wading pool into the garden.

Note: Avoid water from the toilet or kitchen sink (it may contain pathogens) as well as any water containing harsh detergents, cleaners, solvents, pesticides, or other chemicals.

a day. Not just any plumbing will do, however. Gray-water irrigation is closely monitored in arid western states that may have municipal or department of health plumbing codes strictly governing gray-water use.

Recycling once-used water makes it work twice as hard, but gray water may not produce the same glowing results as rain or tap water. In a recent article in GMPRO, a Florida-based nursery discussed how disease pathogens slipped through irrigation-system filters and caused problems with its nursery stock. Compared to the side of the nursery watered with well water, the side irrigated with gray water required more than twice as much spraying and other treatments and still looked inferior.

Potted plants and seedlings in peat-planting mixes can be particularly sensitive to the salts and chemicals accumulated in recycled water. Garden soil, in contrast, acts as a buffer and biofilter, capturing or neutralizing occasional influxes of wastes. To make use of this capability, specialized plumbing systems, installed by a professional, apply gray water underground through a submerged perforated pipe. Like in-ground irrigation, the piping can be zoned for rotating gray water to different parts of the garden. Including an on-off switch makes it possible to choose whether to water with fresh or gray water.

Gray water is recommended only for certain landscape areas and should be applied as soon as it is collected to prevent the buildup of bacteria and fungi in stagnant water.

• Do use it on stay-put ornamental perennials or woody plants that can absorb and immobilize contaminants. If gray water is alkaline, don't use it on acid-loving plants such as rhododendrons and azaleas (*Rhododendron* spp.).

• Avoid using it on edible plants such as vegetables, herbs, and fruit trees and bushes.

• Keep it away from lawns, where it might run off into the nearby watershed and spread diseases or parasites.

• Don't water annual beds with it; contaminants may escape when the soil is vacant or tilled.

When handled carefully, gray water can save the day in droughts with severe water shortages. But it must be treated cautiously and conscientiously to keep gardens healthy and the environment uncontaminated.

WATER-
CONSERVING
PLANTS

W ater in its purest form has the same physical and chemical properties wherever it is found. But the thousands of species of plants worldwide, all of which drink water to survive and thrive, are unique individuals. A cabbage plant, for instance, absorbs and releases 518 pounds of water to produce a 1-pound cabbage head. Cantaloupes transpire more than three times as much: 1,754 pounds of water to produce a 1-pound melon. Potatoes use and lose over 2,000 pounds of water for 1 pound of tubers.

Understanding that the water appetites of plants differ is at the root of a water-conserving landscape. Employing the most frugal water users for dry climates and soils or easy-natured, drought-tolerant plants for occasional dry spells in moister regions allows gardeners to produce an eye-pleasing garden of robust plants with little help from the garden hose.

Exploring the drought tolerance and durability of different plants is part of the art of gardening, and it can reveal new ways of saving water. Try planting a perennial in a moist and a dry garden. Some species may actually perform better in the dry garden, staying more compact and sturdy than in moister soil. Experiment with an established shrub: let it go without water for several weeks during a drought to see if it can be self-supporting. If it has rooted deeply enough or is growing in naturally rich, moist soil, it may handle lean conditions without a problem.

In *Aristocrats of the Garden*, plant explorer Ernest Wilson called gardening a fine sport: "The zest is equal to that of any other game extant. Those fond of a harmless little gamble (and who is not?) may indulge in the fascinating sport of testing the hardiness, adaptability, and garden value of . . . plants. . . . It is all in the game of garden-making."

Drought-tolerant plants adapt in several different ways; it is helpful to know how they survive when planning a water-conserving landscape. Some are from arid regions—deserts, chaparrals, and prairies—and have adapted their leaves, roots, and habit over time to use water efficiently. From South Africa, with its prolonged droughts and dry veld grasslands, comes the hardy, pink ice plant (*Delosperma cooperi*) with succulent, water-holding leaves. The poor, dry soils of the Mediterranean have spawned early-blooming, gray-leaved basket of gold (*Aurinia saxatilis*) and silver-leaved lavender cotton (*Santolina chamaecyparissus*).

Other good-natured, adaptable species are able to tolerate, or even thrive, in a wide range of conditions. For example, the common hackberry (*Celtis occidentalis*) grows from moist creekside flood plains to the dry berms of roads, sunny fields, and the partly shaded edges of woodlands—a range encompassing moderately wet to very dry soils.

The malleable nature that makes some plants able to adapt to their surroundings is particularly useful in regions that have both moist and dry weather. But adaptable plants may come with some strings attached. Because they grow easily in many situations, plants such as bachelor's button (*Centaurea cyanus*), green ash (*Fraxinus pennsylvanica*), and black-eyed Susans (*Rudbeckia hirta*), may spread aggressively to the point of becoming weedy.

A third class of plants prefer moist, rich soil but once well established will be able to tolerate occasional droughts. Plants of this type, including mature, thriving lilacs (*Syringa vulgaris*), are ideal for ordinarily mesic regions that suffer from occasional dry spells.

All water-conserving plants will need some watering at the start. In moist soils the young roots can spread far and wide, preparing the plant to handle later droughts. In dry climates or dry seasons, it is folly to attempt to test drought tolerance before a young plant settles into an irrigated setting.

MAKING THE MOST OF SPRING RAINS

Some annuals, perennials, and bulbs flower during the moist spring season and go dormant during dry times of summer, almost eliminating the need for watering. Trilliums (*Trillium* spp.), Virginia bluebells (*Mertensia virginica*), daffodils (*Narcissus* spp.), tulips (*Tulipa* spp.), and old-fashioned bleeding heart (*Dicentra spectabilis*) provide good examples of this alternative for a water-saving garden.

All three kinds of water-conserving plants are described in the Encyclopedia of Low- to Moderate-Water-Use Plants that follows.

ENCYCLOPEDIA OF LOW- TO MODERATE-WATER-USE PLANTS

Herbs, vegetables and fruits, annuals, perennials, vines and ground covers, shrubs, and trees suitable for water-conserving gardens are listed in this section. Each plant is provided with quick-reference ratings on Water Use, Hardiness, Site, Characteristics, and Landscape Use.

All plants in this encyclopedia are low or moderate water users. Where appropriate, this section notes whether plants are adaptable, require lean conditions, or tolerate occasional dryness and drought.

Hardiness ratings, based on the United States Department of Agriculture Hardiness Zone Map, provide a range of cold and heat tolerance, which allows gardeners to determine whether a plant will survive summer and winter in the backyard. Instead of using hardiness zones, annuals are described as *warm season*, growing during frost-free weather, and *cool season*, tolerating frost. A few annuals are tender perennials, suitable for potting and bringing indoors in winter in cold climates.

Under "Site," look for details on soil conditions and sun exposure that will encourage the best growth and establishment. Plants that need sun require full sun most of the day, while those suited for light shade might have bright dappled sunlight or a half-day of sun. Plants for partial shade might have a few hours of morning or afternoon sun.

Soil described as well-drained will shed excess water quickly. A sharply drained soil loses excess moisture even more promptly, within minutes. A lean soil may be sandy or rocky and tends to be dry and low in nutrients. A rich soil will be fertile, with a high organic content. A moist soil will hold generous water reserves.

LOCAL ALTERNATIVES

In addition to the plants listed here, some regionally adapted plants are ideally suited to a water-saving garden, particularly one in arid parts of the western United States. According to the Arizona Nursery Association, for instance, xeriscaping favorites for Arizona include paloverde (*Cercidium* spp.), desert willow (*Chilopsis* spp.), bird-of-paradise (*Caesalpinia* spp.), sage (*Leucophyllum* spp.), yellowbells (*Tecoma* spp.), and red yucca (*Hesperaloe* spp.).

Consult your local Cooperative Extension Service, botanical garden, or arboretum to find out more about water-conserving plants for your region.

"Characteristics" provides a portrait of the ornamental qualities of the plant—foliage, form, flowers, and fruit—all of which are important for an attractive design.

"Landscape Use" gives ideas on the kinds of gardens in which to use each plant. Many are suitable for multiple gardens, their repetition being one way to provide rhythm and continuity to a landscape design. No plant stands alone and all should be interrelated through the expanse of the yard.

Plants are listed alphabetically by botanical name except for the section on vegetables and fruits, which are listed alphabetically by common name. Botanical names are based on *Hortus Third*, with more recent changes in nomenclature listed as synonyms.

HERBS: Herbs are plants that work twice as hard as those that merely look good. They flavor cuisine and teas, perfume sachets and potpourri, yield beneficial compounds for medicines, and can be used for decorating. Many of the classic herbs—lavender (*Lavandula* spp.), rosemary (*Rosmarinus officinalis*), fennel (*Foeniculum vulgare*), and thyme (*Thymus* spp.)—hail from dry Mediterranean regions, making them ideal for water-conserving gardens.

Fennel, for instance, has fine feathery leaves that minimize water loss from transpiration; its deep taproot digs down into the cool, moist soil depths. Lavender and rosemary have water-conserving, leathery needlelike leaves that won't waste water. Sun reflective, silver-leaved herbs like artemisia (*Artemisia* spp.) and lavender cotton (*Santolina Chamaecyparissus*) insist on well-drained, lean soil and full sun. These interesting foliar effects make herbs naturals for an herb garden and good mixers in kitchen gardens or flower borders.

Artemisia or White Sage

(Artemisia ludoviciana)

WATER USE: Low, tolerates drought

HARDINESS: Zones 3 to 9

SITE: Sun and well-drained soil

CHARACTERISTICS: This vigorous-growing herb can spread on quickly creeping rhizomes to make large clumps and roaming satellite colonies. It has handsome, narrow, silver leaves that make a bright accent or backdrop 2 to 4 feet high.

LANDSCAPE USE: Cutting garden, herb garden, perennial garden

Silvermound artemisia

(Artemisia schmidtiana 'Nana' or 'Silvermound')*

WATER USE: Low, tolerates drought

HARDINESS: Zones 3 to 7

SITE: Sun and lean, sharply drained soil

CHARACTERISTICS: With finely cut silver leaves, this handsome plant makes neat mounds 1 to 2 feet high. The tidy shape is retained best in dry soils with modest fertility.

LANDSCAPE USE: Edging, container, herb garden, perennial garden, rock garden

Fennel

(*Foeniculum vulgare*)

WATER USE: Low to moderate, tolerates drought

HARDINESS: Zones 5 to 9

SITE: Sun and well-drained soil

CHARACTERISTICS: This slim, upright plant has fine, threadlike, licorice-flavored leaves of bronze or green that make feathery sprays along the 4-foot-tall main stem. The stem is topped with umbrella-shaped clusters of yellow flowers in summer.

LANDSCAPE USE: Herb garden, accent in flower garden

Lavender

(*Lavandula angustifolia*)

WATER USE: Low, tolerates drought

HARDINESS: Zones 5 to 9

SITE: Sun and lean, sharply drained soil

CHARACTERISTICS: This small shrub, famous for the lovely fragrance of its flower buds, also has attractive and aromatic silver, needlelike leaves. It grows in open mounds from 1 to 3 feet high and bears spikes of lavender, blue, or pink flowers in summer.

LANDSCAPE USE: Herb garden, edging, low hedge, accent foliage in flower garden

Oregano

(*Origanum vulgare*)

WATER USE: Moderate, tolerates drought

HARDINESS: Zones 4 to 9

SITE: Sun and well-drained to average soil

CHARACTERISTICS: This creeping to clump-forming perennial grows to 30 inches high. The rounded leaves can be fragrant, flavorful, or plain. Some forms have golden leaves and spread like a low ground cover. In summer, stems are topped with clusters of pink or white flowers, some of which dry easily for everlasting arrangements.

LANDSCAPE USE: Herb garden, edging, ground cover, flower border, mixed vegetable garden

Rosemary

(*Rosmarinus officinalis*)

WATER USE: Low to moderate, tolerates drought

HARDINESS: Zones 8 to 10

SITE: Sun and well-drained soil

CHARACTERISTICS: Boldly flavored needlelike leaves cover the branches of this 2- to 4-foot-high shrub. Some forms stay much lower, bearing creeping or cascading branches. The flowers, borne along most of the branches, are usually blue, but some forms come in pink.

LANDSCAPE USE: Herb or kitchen garden, low hedge, container, hanging basket, edging

Sage

(*Salvia officinalis*)

WATER USE: Low to moderate, tolerates drought

HARDINESS: Zones 3 or 4 to 9

SITE: Sun and lean, sharply drained soil

CHARACTERISTICS: The classic flavoring for Thanksgiving turkey dressing comes from an open, silver-leaved shrub about 2½ feet high, although more compact forms are available.

Sage is also available in less flavorful and less hardy forms with golden, purple, or pink, green, and white leaves. In spring or summer, sage bears showy spikes of purple-blue flowers.

LANDSCAPE USE: Ornamental edible garden, herb garden, container, flower garden

Santolina or lavender cotton
(*Santolina Chamaecyparissus*)

WATER USE: Low, tolerates drought

HARDINESS: Zones 6 to 9

SITE: Sun and lean, sharply drained soil

CHARACTERISTICS: Beautiful, low, gray mounds of furry, silver, divided leaves are the trademark of this plant. In summer, the neat mounds are broken by upright stems of button-shaped, yellow flowers, which some people like to remove to better enjoy the foliage. Lavender cotton grows 1 to 2 feet high and can spread as wide as 4 feet across.

LANDSCAPE USE: Low hedge, herb garden, edging, foliage accent, ground cover

Winter savory
(*Satureja montana*)

WATER USE: Low to moderate, tolerates drought

HARDINESS: Zones 5 to 9

SITE: Sun and well-drained soil

CHARACTERISTICS: Needlelike leaves with delightful aroma and flavor cover fine stems on this low, mounded plant, that grows up to 18 inches high. In summer, pastel pink flowers open in small clusters on the branch tips.

LANDSCAPE USE: Edging, herb and kitchen gardens

Lamb's ears
(*Stachys byzantina*)

WATER USE: Low, tolerates drought

HARDINESS: Zones 4 to 9

SITE: Sun and lean to average, well-drained soil

CHARACTERISTICS: Reputedly once used to bandage wounds, the furry gray leaves of this perennial look like their namesake. They grow in spreading, ground-hugging clusters about 6 inches high. In spring, all but the flowerless varieties used for ground covers bear woolly upright spikes of purple flowers that reach up to 2 feet tall.

LANDSCAPE USE: Edging, ground cover, foliage accent, herb and flower gardens

Common thyme
(*Thymus vulgaris*)

WATER USE: Low to moderate, tolerates drought

HARDINESS: Zones 4 to 9

SITE: Sun and well-drained soil

CHARACTERISTICS: Small rounded to narrow, fragrant, and flavorful leaves cover creeping to mounded shrubs reaching 12 inches high. Cultivars come with leaves of green, gray, or variegation of silver or gold. Small pink or white flowers cover the stems in late spring or early summer, making an attractive display.

LANDSCAPE USE: Edging, ground cover, kitchen and herb gardens, perennial garden, container

Mother-of-thyme
(*Thymus Serpyllum*)

See page 125.

CRITICAL TIMES FOR IRRIGATION

To ensure a good harvest and many healthy returns during drying times, be certain to irrigate vegetables and fruits during critical stages.

CROP	CRITICAL STAGE
Asparagus	fern growth
Bean, snap	pod filling
Broccoli, cabbage, and cauliflower	seedling establishment and head development
Carrot	seedling establishment and root development
Corn	tasseling, silking, and ear filling
Cucumber	flowering and fruit enlargement
Eggplant	flowering and fruit development
Lettuce	head development
Muskmelon	flowering and fruit enlargement
Onion	bulb enlargement
Pea	flowering and pod filling
Pepper	transplanting, fruit set and development
Squash, pumpkins	flowering and fruit development
Tomato	flowering, fruit set and enlargement
Turnip	root enlargement

VEGETABLES AND FRUITS: Well-grown vegetables usually demand evenly moist soil and at least occasional irrigation. If tormented with alternating moist and dry soil, carrots and onion skins may split, lettuce may develop brown leaf tips, and tomatoes may produce scabby brown blossom end rot at the base of the fruit. How well vegetables and fruits withstand occasional dry spells depends a great deal on their root depth, which is calculated here from plants grown in a deep, loose soil. In these ideal situations, as well as in shallower soils, the most active roots remain within the top foot of soil.

Shallow-rooted vegetables like lettuce, celery, radishes, and onions, which develop roots down to 1½ feet deep, suffer quickly when the surface of the soil dries out.

Broccoli, cabbage, cauliflower, Chinese cabbage, and spinach are crops that thrive during cool, moist weather; they root to about 2 feet deep. Warm-season crops with a similar root depth, such as cucumber, muskmelon, and transplanted peppers and tomatoes, are more likely to need irrigation during hot, dry summer months.

Deeper rooters include snap bean, beet, carrot, eggplant, pea, seeded pepper, rutabaga, and summer squash, which can grow 3 to 4 feet deep in loose soil. Even they are surpassed by asparagus, lima bean, parsnip, pumpkin, winter squash, seeded tomato, and watermelon, which are capable of growing roots over 4 feet deep.

There are certain edible crops that can tolerate dry weather once they are established, however. The following are worth considering for a well-drained garden or arid climate. They are listed alphabetically by common name.

Amaranth

(*Amaranthus* spp.)

WATER USE: Moderate, tolerates drought, adaptable

HARDINESS: Warm-season annual

SITE: Sun and rich, fertile soil

CHARACTERISTICS: This versatile and easy-growing crop has leaves to use for salads and steaming and prolific seed heads to use like grain. Plants tend to be upright growers, reaching as high as 4 feet tall and bearing long spikes of inconspicuous flowers. Each plant can produce hundreds of seeds and may become weedy in the garden. A special kind of metabolism lets amaranths grow efficiently in hot, sunny conditions.

LANDSCAPE USE: Vegetable garden

Beans, tepary

(*Phaseolus acutifolius* var. *latifolius*)

WATER USE: Moderate, tolerates drought

HARDINESS: Warm-season annual

SITE: Sun and average soil

CHARACTERISTICS: This native of the arid Southwest is a vining legume that bears 3-inch-long pods of edible beans. The seed coats may be light, dark, or speckled. Harvest before fully dry to catch the beans before they fall to the ground.

LANDSCAPE USE: Vegetable garden

Cherry, Nanking

(*Prunus tomentosa*)

WATER USE: Moderate, tolerates drought

HARDINESS: Zones 2 to 7

SITE: Sun and fertile, well-drained soil

CHARACTERISTICS: Unlike cherry trees, this bush is easy-growing. It reaches 6 to 10 feet high, has white flowers in spring, and red cherries in early to midsummer.

LANDSCAPE USE: Kitchen garden, mixed border, edible ornamental garden

Chestnut, Chinese

(*Castanea mollissima*)

WATER USE: Moderate, tolerates some dryness

HARDINESS: Zones 4 to 8 or 9

SITE: Sun and rich, well-drained soil

CHARACTERISTICS: Harvest chestnuts from this magnificent tree, which reaches 40 to 60 feet tall. It has elliptical toothed leaves that turn yellow or bronze in fall. In late spring, clusters of yellowish flowers emerge and turn into prickly podded nuts. Unlike the American chestnut, this species resists the devastating chestnut blight.

LANDSCAPE USE: Orchard, shade tree located where falling nuts will cause no damage or inconvenience

Turkish Filbert

(*Corylus Colurna*)

See page 131.

Jerusalem artichokes

(*Helianthus tuberosus*)

WATER USE: Moderate, adaptable

HARDINESS: Zones 2 to 9

SITE: Sun and moist, average, or well-drained soil

CHARACTERISTICS: This perennial sunflower produces lumpy underground tubers with a water chestnut flavor. The plants may reach 8 to 12 feet tall and sometimes bear small, golden sunflowers. Jerusalem artichokes tend to spread aggressively, as each tuber can sprout into new plants.

LANDSCAPE USE: Vegetable garden, hedge, isolation bed (to limit spread)

Peppers, chiltepíns

(*Capsicum annuum* var. *glabriusculum*)

WATER USE: Moderate, tolerates drought

HARDINESS: Warm-season annual or tender perennial

SITE: Sun and average to rich soil

CHARACTERISTICS: This native of the arid Southwest is a low shrub growing to 3 feet high. It has small leaves, white flowers, and *very* hot tiny red fruit.

LANDSCAPE USE: Vegetable garden, container

ANNUALS: Annuals are plants that provide a display of flowers or, in some cases, attractive foliage the same year they are planted. Many are colorful throughout the growing season, particularly during warm, frost-free periods, while others may only put on a show for a few months or a few weeks.

When it comes to water-conserving annuals, there are a great many forms, fashions, and colors from which to choose. Use them to paint broad strokes of color across landscape beds. Start the seeds at home, allow self-sowing, or go to a favorite nursery with a large selection, as some of these are out-of-the-ordinary plants. It is important to water annual seedlings to get them off to a strong start. After that point, the following annuals will do well in drier conditions.

Vinca or Madagascar periwinkle

(*Catharanthus roseus*)

WATER USE: Moderate, tolerates some dryness

HARDINESS: Warm-season annual

SITE: Sun and average soil

CHARACTERISTICS: Choose from upright, bushy forms ideal for bedding or trailing types for hanging baskets and containers. Both have shiny green leaves and five-parted flowers that can reach to 2 inches across. Cultivars flower in pink, lavender, white, rose, and apricot, sometimes with a contrasting colored eye.

LANDSCAPE USE: Bedding, ground cover, container, edging

Cockscomb

(*Celosia cristata*)

WATER USE: Moderate, tolerates some dryness, moderately adaptable

HARDINESS: Warm-season annual

SITE: Sun and average to rich soil

CHARACTERISTICS: This annual flower, which comes in several forms, may have plume-shaped or crest-shaped flowers in gold, red, yellow, pink, orange, and pastels. A similar cockscomb (*Celosia spicata*) has feather-shaped flowers. The plants reach 8 to 30 inches tall, varying with the cultivar.

LANDSCAPE USE: Flower border, annual bedding, edging, cutting garden, container

Bachelor's button or cornflower

(*Centaurea cyanus*)

WATER USE: Moderate, tolerates drought, adaptable

HARDINESS: Cool- or warm-season annual

SITE: Sun and well-drained to average soil

CHARACTERISTICS: Bright heads of blue, pink, red, maroon, lavender, or white flowers grow at the top of 1- to 3-foot-tall upright plants with narrow gray-green leaves. When the bloom is through, they quickly go to seed and may be removed from the garden.

Sowing new seeds in succession through spring and early summer extends the bloom time.

LANDSCAPE USE: Informal or naturalized garden, cutting garden

Spider flower

(*Cleome hasslerana*)

WATER USE: Moderate, tolerates drought

HARDINESS: Warm-season annual

SITE: Sun or light shade, average to rich soil

CHARACTERISTICS: The flowers of this annual inspire its name. Borne in open clusters, they have white, pink, lavender, or purple petals and long-legged stamens. They reach 3 to 5 feet tall and have sticky, five- to seven-parted compound leaves.

LANDSCAPE USE: Background flower, hedge, mixed flower garden

Calliopsis or tickseed

(*Coreopsis tinctoria*)

WATER USE: Low to moderate, tolerates drought, adaptable

HARDINESS: Warm-season annual

SITE: Sun and well-drained soil

CHARACTERISTICS: This American native has toothed, daisylike flowers that are naturally bicolored yellow with brown centers and also available in orange, red, or mahogany. They grow upright, reach 1 to 3 feet tall, and have narrow leaves. The plants will rebloom all summer if the old flowers are removed.

LANDSCAPE USE: Bedding, mixed flower border, cutting garden

Cosmos

(*Cosmos bipinnatus*)

WATER USE: Low to moderate, tolerates drought

HARDINESS: Warm-season annual

SITE: Sun and lean, well-drained soil

CHARACTERISTICS: Feathery, emerald leaves cover upright plants that reach 2 to 5 feet tall, depending on the cultivar, and are topped with abundant pink, rose, or white daisylike flowers. Drier soils of limited fertility encourage taller plants to stand without extra support.

LANDSCAPE USE: Flower garden, mixed border, cottage garden, cutting garden

California poppy

(*Eschscholzia californica*)

WATER USE: Low to moderate, tolerates drought

HARDINESS: Cool-season annual or short-lived perennial

SITE: Sun to light shade and well-drained soil

CHARACTERISTICS: This California wildflower is well suited for dry gardens. It has divided blue-green leaves and open-faced flowers of golden orange on 12- to 15-inch-high stems. Cultivars come with flowers of white, rose, scarlet, crimson, and salmon.

LANDSCAPE USE: Flower border, rock garden, naturalized meadow

Snow-on-the-mountain

(*Euphorbia marginata*)

WATER USE: Low to moderate, adaptable

HARDINESS: Warm-season annual

SITE: Sun and well-drained soil

CHARACTERISTICS: This annual is grown for its white-margined leaves, which develop in decorative clusters at the tips of the stems. It grows into an upright bush 1 to 3 feet high, and is best handled with gloves because the milky sap can irritate unprotected skin.

LANDSCAPE USE: Mixed flower garden, low hedge

Blanketflower

(*Gaillardia pulchella*)

WATER USE: Low to moderate, tolerates drought

HARDINESS: Warm-season annual

SITE: Sun and well-drained soil

CHARACTERISTICS: This flashy native wildflower has daisylike heads, usually bicolored yellow and red. Cultivars are available in single colors of orange, red, or yellow and double-flowered forms. The plants grow 1 to 2 feet tall and have narrow leaves and long flower stems.

LANDSCAPE USE: Mixed flower border, naturalized meadow, cottage garden, cutting garden

Globe amaranth

(*Gomphrena globosa* and *Gomphrena Haageana*)

WATER USE: Moderate, tolerates drought, adaptable

HARDINESS: Warm-season annual

SITE: Sun and well-drained soil

CHARACTERISTICS: This easy grower has ball-shaped clusters of purple, red, pink, lavender, white, yellow, or orange flowers, all suitable for cutting and drying. The leaves are oblong and plants grow from 8 to 30 inches high, depending on the cultivar.

LANDSCAPE USE: Edging, bedding, border, cutting garden, container

Lantana

(*Lantana camara*)

WATER USE: Low to moderate

HARDINESS: Warm-season annual or tender perennial

SITE: Sun and well-drained soil

CHARACTERISTICS: This tropical American shrub can reach 3 to 15 feet high and also comes in low-spreading forms. It has large-toothed leaves and bears stunning clusters of white, yellow, gold, orange, or red flowers, often with two colors per cluster.

LANDSCAPE USE: Container, back of flower bed, hanging basket, ground cover

Golden ageratum or African daisy

(*Lonas inodora*)

WATER USE: Low to moderate

HARDINESS: Warm-season annual

SITE: Sun and well-drained soil

CHARACTERISTICS: This Mediterranean flower has clusters of powder puff–shaped, yellow blossoms on plants reaching to 1 foot high. The leaves are divided and petite.

LANDSCAPE USE: Flower border, informal mixed border, cutting garden

Moss rose or portulaca

(*Portulaca grandiflora*)

WATER USE: Low, tolerates drought

HARDINESS: Warm-season annual

SITE: Sun and well-drained soil

CHARACTERISTICS: This Brazilian native, with succulent, needle-shaped leaves and fleshy stems, grows in low mats or mounds. The open-faced flowers come in single and double forms and colors such as yellow, gold, orange, red, purple, pink, and white.

LANDSCAPE USE: Flower-garden edging, bedding, container, rock garden, between stones in walks or patios

Gloriosa daisy or black-eyed Susan

(*Rudbeckia hirta*)

WATER USE: Low to moderate, tolerates drought, moderately adaptable

HARDINESS: Cool- and warm-season annual

SITE: Sun and average or rich, well-drained soil

CHARACTERISTICS: This prairie wildflower is a short-lived perennial masquerading as an annual since it blooms the first year after sowing. It has furry leaves and long flower stems holding daisylike blossoms of gold, bronze, and mahogany, as well as gold-tipped bicolor combinations. Plants grow from 1 to 3 feet tall.

LANDSCAPE USE: Bed, border, naturalized garden, cutting garden

Sanvitalia or creeping zinnia

(*Sanvitalia procumbens*)

WATER USE: Low to moderate, tolerates drought

HARDINESS: Warm-season annual

SITE: Sun and well-drained soil of moderate fertility

CHARACTERISTICS: This creeping annual from arid parts of Mexico has yellow flowers with purple or brown centers, like a black-eyed Susan. They are small but prolific. Sanvitalia reaches only 6 inches high but can spread to 18 inches across.

LANDSCAPE USE: Bedding, border, edging, rock garden, container, hanging basket

Mexican sunflower or tithonia

(*Tithonia rotundifolia*)

WATER USE: Low to moderate, tolerates drought

HARDINESS: Warm-season annual

SITE: Sun and well-drained soil

CHARACTERISTICS: This Mexican annual is an eye-catcher. It grows from 3 to 8 feet tall, depending on the cultivar, and bears vivid, daisylike flowers of reddish orange or yellow. The hairy leaves can be toothed or lobed.

LANDSCAPE USE: Back of the border, temporary screen, butterfly garden

Moss verbena

(*Verbena tenuisecta*)

WATER USE: Low to moderate, tolerates drought

HARDINESS: Warm-season annual or tender perennial

SITE: Sun and well-drained soil

CHARACTERISTICS: This South American creeper reaches about 1 foot high and has dainty divided leaflets and showy clusters of small purple, lilac, white, or blue flowers, depending on the cultivar.

LANDSCAPE USE: Ground cover, rock garden, container, front of flower bed, edging

Brazilian verbena

(*Verbena bonariensis*)

WATER USE: Low to moderate, tolerates drought

HARDINESS: Warm-season annual or tender perennial

SITE: Sun to light shade and well-drained soil

CHARACTERISTICS: Dense clusters of small lavender or purple flowers top upright stems reaching 3 to 4 feet high. The leaves are elliptical and toothed.

LANDSCAPE USE: Flower garden, mixed border

PERENNIALS: Mostly herbaceous flowers that live several years or longer, perennials may not bloom all summer as many annuals do. Instead, they often peak in spring, summer, or fall. This opens up many options for creating a constantly changing perennial garden with new colors, textures, and plant combinations showing up every season.

A great variety of perennials, once well established, thrive in airy, dry soils and tolerate drought.

Fern-leaved yarrow

(*Achillea filipendulina*)

WATER USE: Low to moderate, tolerates drought

HARDINESS: Zones 3 to 9

SITE: Sun and well-drained soil

CHARACTERISTICS: Above basal rosettes of feathery leaves, umbrella-shaped heads of golden flowers stretch to 4 feet high in summer. Even a small nursery plant can spread 3 to 4 feet wide and colonize surrounding areas.

LANDSCAPE USE: Perennial garden, mixed border, cutting garden

Common yarrow

(*Achillea millefolium*)

WATER USE: Low to moderate, tolerates drought, adaptable

HARDINESS: Zones 3 to 9

SITE: Sun and well-drained soil

CHARACTERISTICS: This Eurasian wildflower now grows wild along roadsides, in meadows, and even through lawns across most of the United States, attesting to its adaptability. Cultivated counterparts make attractive garden plants. Clusters of delicate, finely cut foliage hug the ground while in summer flat-topped heads of white, pink, or red flowers stretch up on sometimes floppy stems 1 to 2½ feet tall.

LANDSCAPE USE: Flower border, cutting garden, naturalized garden

Anthemis or marguerite

(*Anthemis tinctoria*)

WATER USE: Low to moderate, tolerates drought

HARDINESS: Zones 3 to 7

SITE: Sun and well-drained soil

CHARACTERISTICS: Moderate-sized, yellow, daisylike flowers appear in summer. Marguerite, which has strongly fragrant divided leaves, can grow 1 to 3 feet high but is likely to sprawl in moist and fertile soils.

LANDSCAPE USE: Perennial garden, rock garden, container

Common thrift

(*Armeria maritima*)

WATER USE: Low to moderate, moderately adaptable

HARDINESS: Zones 4 to 8

SITE: Sun and well-drained soil

CHARACTERISTICS: This plant thrives in sandy and salty seaside locations and also tolerates clay. It has neat mats of grasslike foliage topped in late spring and early summer with ball-shaped clusters of pink, rose, red, and white flowers. The flower color varies with the cultivar.

LANDSCAPE USE: Edging, rock garden, perennial and mixed borders

Butterfly weed

(*Asclepias tuberosa*)

WATER USE: Low to moderate, tolerates drought

HARDINESS: Zones 3 to 8

SITE: Sun and well-drained soil

CHARACTERISTICS: A prairie wildflower with a deep taproot, this plant bears ball-like clusters of orange flowers in midsummer. Cultivars come with red or yellow flowers as well. The flowers are followed by attractive upright pods. The plant reaches 1 to 1½ feet high and has neat, narrow leaves.

LANDSCAPE USE: Flower garden, mixed border, wildlife garden, naturalized garden, prairie garden

Blue false indigo

(*Baptisia australis*)

WATER USE: Moderate, tolerates drought, moderately adaptable

HARDINESS: Zones 3 to 8

SITE: Sun to light shade, rich to well-drained soil

CHARACTERISTICS: Once grown to yield a blue dye similar to indigo, this 2- to 4-foot-tall perennial has a deep taproot and spikes of blue lupinelike flowers in spring or early summer. They are followed by dark seed pods, also of ornamental interest. The leaves are clover-shaped and handsome in their own right.

LANDSCAPE USE: Perennial or mixed flower garden, mixed border, meadow garden

Poppy mallow

(*Callirhoe involucrata*)

WATER USE: Low to moderate

HARDINESS: Zones 4 to 7

SITE: Sun and well-drained soil

CHARACTERISTICS: Open-faced purple flowers cover mostly prostrate stems from early summer into autumn. The divided leaves are also attractive. Plants reach 6 to 12 inches high and can spread to 3 feet across. Self-sown seedlings can be common.

LANDSCAPE USE: Rock garden, flower garden, edging, cascading accent, ground cover, naturalized garden

Centranthus or red valerian

(Centranthus ruber)

WATER USE: Moderate, adaptable

HARDINESS: Zones 5 to 8

SITE: Sun and well-drained soil

CHARACTERISTICS: Showy clusters of small red, pink, rose, or white flowers top stems of blue-green leaves in late spring and, sometimes, again in mid-summer. Plants often reach 3 feet tall and frequently self-sow.

LANDSCAPE USE: Flower garden, rock garden, naturalized garden, cutting garden

Mouse-ear chickweed or cerastium

(Cerastium tomentosum)

WATER USE: Low to moderate, tolerates drought

HARDINESS: Zones 2 to 7

SITE: Sun and well- to sharply drained soil

CHARACTERISTICS: This silver-leaved spring bloomer erupts with an avalanche of white flowers. The petals are divided at the tip like those of its relative chickweed. Mouse-ear chickweed is a mat former that grows to 10 inches tall and spreads aggressively. Limited fertilizer and water suit this plant well.

LANDSCAPE USE: Rock garden, wall, edging, bank, container, flower garden, mixed border, ground cover

Lance-leaved coreopsis

(Coreopsis lanceolata)

WATER USE: Moderate, adaptable

HARDINESS: Zones 3 to 8

SITE: Sun and average to rich, well-drained soil

CHARACTERISTICS: Bright golden daisylike flowers top medium-sized plants 1 to 2 feet tall. The flowers appear through summer and fall, especially if old flowers are faithfully removed. Large-flowered coreopsis (*Coreopsis grandiflora*), which looks similar, also can be useful in a water-conserving garden.

LANDSCAPE USE: Flower garden, prairie garden, mixed border

Thread-leaved coreopsis

(Coreopsis verticillata)

WATER USE: Moderate, tolerates drought

HARDINESS: Zones 5 to 9

SITE: Sun and well-drained soil

CHARACTERISTICS: The yellow or gold daisylike flowers on thread-leaved coreopsis are smaller than those of lance-leaved coreopsis but appear in greater abundance. If deadheaded, thread-leaved coreopsis will flower most of summer and into fall. The plant has fine, threadlike leaves and a graceful rounded shape, reaching 18 to 36 inches high, depending on the cultivar.

LANDSCAPE USE: Perennial garden, mixed border, naturalized garden

Ice plant

(Delosperma cooperi and *Delosperma nubigenum)*

WATER USE: Low

HARDINESS: Zones 5 or 7 to 10

SITE: Sun and sharply drained soil

CHARACTERISTICS: These natives of arid South Africa have bright pink or golden daisylike flowers from spring into summer. They spread across the ground, reaching only about 6 inches high, and have narrow, succulent leaves that may turn purple in fall.

LANDSCAPE USE: Ground cover, rock garden, slope, perennial garden

Dianthus or pinks

(*Dianthus* spp.)

WATER USE: Low to moderate

HARDINESS: Zones 3 or 4 to 8 or 9

SITE: Sun and well-drained soil

CHARACTERISTICS: Most pinks are alike in having fragrant flowers with petal edges that look like they have been trimmed with pinking shears. Naturally low growers, they form clumps and mats of green or grayish foliage.

LANDSCAPE USE: Rock garden, edging, flower garden, cottage garden, gaps in flagstones

Purple coneflower

(*Echinacea purpurea*)

WATER USE: Moderate, tolerates drought, adaptable

HARDINESS: Zones 3 to 8

SITE: Sun and well-drained soil

CHARACTERISTICS: Large daisylike flowers with purple florets surrounding a central orange cone are the trademark of this species. Cultivars are also available with flowers of rose, mauve, or white. The leaves grow primarily in ground-hugging rosettes while the flowers stretch up on 2- to 4-foot-high stems. Bloom peaks in summer and may last into fall.

LANDSCAPE USE: Perennial garden, mixed border, naturalized garden, cutting garden

Globe thistle

(*Echinops ritro*)

WATER USE: Low to moderate, tolerates drought

HARDINESS: Zones 3 to 7

SITE: Sun and well-drained soil

CHARACTERISTICS: In summer, globelike clusters of small blue flowers appear over prickly bracts. Plants can reach 2 to 4 feet tall, have long, spiny leaves, and are anchored by a taproot.

LANDSCAPE USE: Perennial garden, cutting garden

Sulphur flower

(*Eriogonum umbellatum*)

WATER USE: Low to very low, tolerates drought

HARDINESS: Zones 4 to 8

SITE: Full sun and sharply drained soil

CHARACTERISTICS: A shrubby perennial native to the Rockies, sulphur flower produces clusters of cream to yellow flowers in summer. The leaves, which are furry below, stay in ground-hugging rosettes while the flowers can reach to 12 inches high.

LANDSCAPE USE: Edging, rock garden, cutting garden

Sea holly

(*Eryngium* spp.)

WATER USE: Low to moderate, tolerates drought

HARDINESS: Zones 4 or 5 to 7 or 8

SITE: Sun and sharply drained to average soil

CHARACTERISTICS: This taprooted group of rugged perennials bears globes of blue flowers with decorative silver to purple bracts below. The leaves vary from divided to heart-shaped, depending on the species. Most grow 1 to 2 feet tall, although giant sea holly (*Eryngium giganteum*) reaches 4 to 6 feet tall.

LANDSCAPE USE: Perennial garden, cutting garden

Blanketflower

(*Gaillardia* × *grandiflora*)

WATER USE: Low to moderate, tolerates drought, adaptable

HARDINESS: Zones 4 to 9

SITE: Sun and well-drained soil

CHARACTERISTICS: Somewhat similar to its annual counterpart (see page 113), this perennial has daisylike flowers of yellow often with a maroon or red eye and toothed petal edges. Some cultivars have solid yellow or red flowers. Blanket flowers may bloom from summer through fall and reach 1 to 3 feet tall. The toothed foliage is tinted gray.

LANDSCAPE USE: Perennial garden, mixed border

Endres cranesbill

(*Geranium endressii*)

WATER USE: Moderate, tolerates drought

HARDINESS: Zones 4 to 8

SITE: Sun or light shade and rich, well-drained soil

CHARACTERISTICS: Pretty divided leaves cover mounded 15- to 18-inch-high plants. They are topped with open-faced flowers of pink, salmon, or lilac in summer.

LANDSCAPE USE: Perennial garden, mixed border

Bigroot cranesbill

(*Geranium macrorrhizum*)

WATER USE: Moderate, tolerates drought, adaptable

HARDINESS: Zones 3 to 8

SITE: Sun or partial shade and rich, well-drained soil

CHARACTERISTICS: Thick, questing roots send this ground covering perennial across the garden and support it during dry times. It has aromatic leaves and open-faced pink or rose flowers in spring; the color varies with the cultivar. The plant reaches 15 to 18 inches tall.

LANDSCAPE USE: Flower border, ground cover, mixed border

Bloody cranesbill

(*Geranium sanguineum*)

WATER USE: Moderate, tolerates drought

HARDINESS: Zones 3 to 8

SITE: Sun or partial shade and rich, well-drained soil

CHARACTERISTICS: A neat mound-shaped perennial, bloody cranesbill grows 8 to 12 inches tall, depending on the cultivar. It has finely cut leaves and pink, white, purple, or rose flowers in late spring and early summer.

LANDSCAPE USE: Flower border, edging, mixed border

Daylily

(*Hemerocallis* spp.)

WATER USE: Moderate, adaptable

HARDINESS: Zones 4 to 10

SITE: Sun to light shade and average to

rich, well-drained soil

CHARACTERISTICS: As the name implies, the trumpet-shaped flowers of daylilies last only one day, but the bloom period can extend from several weeks to several months, depending on the number of buds produced. Daylily flowers come in yellow, orange, red, purple, lavender, pink, and cream. The plants can reach 10 inches to 5 feet high, depending on the cultivar. The strap-shaped leaves form upright clumps.

LANDSCAPE USE: Border, ground cover, cutting garden, foundation planting, edible ornamental garden

Missouri evening primrose

(*Oenothera missourensis* syn. *O. macrocarpa*)

WATER USE: Low to moderate, adaptable

HARDINESS: Zones 4 to 7

SITE: Sun to light shade and well-drained soil

CHARACTERISTICS: This Missouri, Kansas, and Texas native has cup-shaped yellow flowers on a compact plant 8 to 12 inches high. Like many other evening primrose species, these summer-blooming flowers open in the evening but stay open in the daytime too. The leaves are elongated. The roots grow deeply and spread horizontally to claim an ever-growing expanse of garden territory.

LANDSCAPE USE: Prairie garden, perennial garden, rock garden, ground cover

Prickly pear

(*Opuntia humifusa* syn. *O. compressa*)

WATER USE: Low, tolerates drought

HARDINESS: Zones 4 to 9

SITE: Sun and well-drained average or sandy soil

CHARACTERISTICS: This hardy cactus has the broad, flat, spiny stems typical of other prickly pear cacti, but it reaches only 4 to 6 inches high. Vivid yellow flowers appear in late spring or summer followed by green or purple fruit.

LANDSCAPE USE: Rock garden, flower garden

Sunset beardtongue

(*Penstemon clutei*)

WATER USE: Low, tolerates drought

HARDINESS: Zones 4 to 9

SITE: Sun and sharply drained soil

CHARACTERISTICS: Native to arid Arizona, sunset beardtongue bears open spikes of pink or purplish flowers from summer into fall. The blue-green foliage may reach only 4 inches high while the flowers rise 3 feet above it.

LANDSCAPE USE: Dry garden, perennial border

Russian sage

(*Perovskia atriplicifolia*)

WATER USE: Low to moderate, tolerates drought

HARDINESS: Zones 5 to 9

SITE: Sun and well-drained soil

CHARACTERISTICS: This upright perennial has handsome gray-green toothed leaves with a fragrance reminiscent of sage. The showy long-lasting sprays of small blue flowers emerge in summer and reach to 4 feet high.

LANDSCAPE USE: Perennial garden, screen, herb garden

Mexican hat

(*Ratibida columnifera*)

WATER USE: Low to moderate, tolerates drought

HARDINESS: Zones 4 to 10

SITE: Sun and well-drained soil

CHARACTERISTICS: Native to periodically dry prairies of North America, Mexican hat produces flowers that resemble golden coneflowers. They differ, however, in having protruding green to brown cones that create the silhouette of a high-crowned Mexican sombrero. The flowers, which reach to 2 feet high, bloom most of the summer. The leaves are finely divided and the taproot grows deep.

LANDSCAPE USE: Cutting garden, prairie garden, meadow garden, perennial border

Orange coneflower

(*Rudbeckia fulgida*)

WATER USE: Moderate, tolerates some dryness

HARDINESS: Zones 3 to 8

SITE: Full sun and average to rich, well-drained soil

CHARACTERISTICS: This prairie native is a favorite perennial because it blooms much of the summer and into fall. The black-eyed, golden orange flowers stretch 12 to 36 inches above rosettes of furry leaves.

LANDSCAPE USE: Perennial border, mixed border, wild garden, shrub border

Stonecrop

(*Sedum* spp.)

WATER USE: Low to moderate, tolerates drought

HARDINESS: Zones 3 or 4 to 7 or 8

SITE: Sun and well-drained soil

CHARACTERISTICS: This diverse group of plants varies from upright, clump-forming perennials like 'Autumn Joy' (*Sedum* 'Autumn Joy') to creepers like goldenmoss stonecrop (*Sedum acre*). All have fleshy, water-conserving leaves and flashy clusters of small flowers.

LANDSCAPE USE: Flower garden, ground cover

Kamschatka sedum

(*Sedum kamtschaticum*)

See page 125.

Hens-and-chicks

(*Sempervivum* spp.)

WATER USE: Low to moderate

HARDINESS: Zones 4 to 8

SITE: Sun to partial shade, well-drained soil

CHARACTERISTICS: These old-fashioned favorites produce rosettes of succulent leaves and identical little offsets, like a hen with her chicks. Clusters of small summer flowers come in white, green, yellow, or red, depending on the species and cultivar. The plants stay 4 to 12 inches high.

LANDSCAPE USE: Container, between gaps in patio or walk, rock garden

Adam's needle

(*Yucca filamentosa*)

WATER USE: Low to moderate, tolerates drought

HARDINESS: Zones 4 or 5 to 9

SITE: Sun and well-drained soil

CHARACTERISTICS: These striking south-western United States natives have upright rosettes of evergreen swordlike leaves; some cultivars are variegated with gold or white. The leaves generally reach 2 to 3 feet tall. Striking stems of white, bell-shaped flowers can rise up to 6 feet high in late spring or summer.

LANDSCAPE USE: Flower garden, shrub bed, rock garden

Golden paperflower

(*Zinnia grandiflora*)

WATER USE: Very low, not for moister gardens

HARDINESS: Zones 4 to 7

SITE: Sun and well-drained soil

CHARACTERISTICS: A native of the arid southwestern United States, this hardy zinnia bursts into papery yellow daisy-like flowers from summer into the fall. The water-conserving leaves are narrow. The plant grows in a low mound, reaching to 8 inches high and spreading to 12 inches wide. It has narrow, water-conserving leaves.

LANDSCAPE USE: Rock garden, bed edging, ground cover

ORNAMENTAL GRASSES: With green, blue, gold, or bronze blades that ripple gracefully in the wind and airy flower and seed plumes, ornamental grasses can be a beautiful addition to the water-conserving garden. Grasses need to be kept moist until well established, but many tolerate dry gardens thereafter. They may, in fact, stay more compact and attractive in lean conditions. Choose from grasses native to your region or from widespread species such as little bluestem (*Schizachyrium scoparium*). To ensure hardiness, grasses are best propagated from local stock.

Big bluestem

(*Andropogon gerardii*)

WATER USE: Low to moderate, tolerates drought

HARDINESS: Zones 4 to 10

SITE: Sun and well-drained soil

CHARACTERISTICS: This prairie grass hrives during warm weather and can reach over 6 feet tall. The leaves can be tinted blue, turning bronze in fall. They are topped by violet spikes of flowers in late summer.

LANDSCAPE USE: Background plant, screen, naturalized garden, prairie garden, perennial garden

Side oats grama

(*Bouteloua curtipendula*)

WATER USE: Low to moderate, tolerates drought, adaptable

HARDINESS: Zones 4 to 8

SITE: Sun and fertile, well-drained soil

CHARACTERISTICS: This decorative grass has clumps of gray-tinted leaves 1 to 2 feet high and one-sided spikes of purple flowers in early summer.

LANDSCAPE USE: Ground cover, accent, meadow, prairie garden, cutting garden, bank

Buffalo grass

(*Buchloe dactyloides*)

WATER USE: Low to moderate, tolerates drought, adaptable

HARDINESS: Zones 4 to 8

SITE: Sun and well-drained soil

CHARACTERISTICS: Short, fine-textured blades reach only 4 to 6 inches high and tolerate mowing. Buffalo grass creeps slowly and stays green during the warm season, turning tan in winter. The root system is deep, extensive, and self-supportive. The flowers are not particularly ornamental.

LANDSCAPE USE: Lawn, ground cover

Blue lyme grass

(*Leymus racemosus* 'Glaucus' syn. *Elymus racemosus* 'Glaucus')

WATER USE: Moderate, adaptable

HARDINESS: Zones 4 to 9

SITE: Sun and well-drained soil

CHARACTERISTICS: This grass hits the garden and begins running, potentially becoming invasive. The leaves are tinted pale blue. The flowers come in summer on upright spikes that reach to 30 inches high.

LANDSCAPE USE: Bank, ground cover, wild garden

Blue fescue

(*Festuca glauca*)

WATER USE: Low, tolerates drought

HARDINESS: Zones 4 to 8

SITE: Sun and well-drained soil

CHARACTERISTICS: Neat tuftlike clumps of blue-green leaves reach to 8 inches high and are topped in summer by spikes of flowers 12 inches high.

LANDSCAPE USE: Rock garden, ground cover, edging, mixed border, containers

Tender fountain grass

(*Pennisetum setaceum*)

WATER USE: Low to moderate, tolerates drought, adaptable

HARDINESS: Zones 8 to 10

SITE: Sun to light shade and well-drained soil

CHARACTERISTICS: Handsome upright clumps of arching green or red bronze leaves reach 3 to 4 feet tall, depending on the cultivar. Red-tinted flowers appear in summer. Self-sown seedlings are common in warm climates.

LANDSCAPE USE: Annual garden, mixed border, natural garden

Feathertop

(*Pennisetum villosum*)

WATER USE: Low to moderate, tolerates drought, adaptable

HARDINESS: Zones 9 to 10

SITE: Sun and average, well-drained soil

CHARACTERISTICS: This grass, native to dry African savannas, has the potential to self-seed aggressively in warm climates. In cold climates, it can safely be grown as an annual. It makes attractive clumps of 1- to 2-foot-high blue-green blades. White flower plumes appear in summer and fall.

LANDSCAPE USE: Bank, ground cover, cutting garden

Little bluestem

(*Schizachyrium scoparium*)

WATER USE: Low to moderate, tolerates drought, moderately adaptable

HARDINESS: Zones 3 to 10

SITE: Sun and well-drained soil

CHARACTERISTICS: A native of American prairies, this well-loved grass has clumps of green foliage that reach 2 feet tall and, in late summer and fall, airy flower plumes that can extend to 3 feet high. The leaves turn red in fall.

LANDSCAPE USE: Masses, naturalizing, perennial garden, cutting garden

Prairie dropseed

(*Sporobolus heterolepis*)

WATER USE: Low, tolerates drought

HARDINESS: Zones 3 to 9

SITE: Sun and well- to sharply drained soil

CHARACTERISTICS: Graceful arching green leaves grow to 2 feet high and change to gold in fall. In late summer, fragrant plumes of flowers reach over 3 feet high.

LANDSCAPE USE: Prairie garden, flower garden, wildlife garden

GROUND COVERS AND VINES: Replacing thirsty lawns with beds of easy care ground covers can save labor and water. The varying leaf textures and flower colors of different ground covers can break up the monotony of too much grass. Some ground covers, such as ivy (*Hedera Helix*), wintercreeper (*Euonymus Fortunei*), and Virginia creeper (*Parthenocissus quinquefolia*), are also vines. They can brighten the trunks of trees, fences, trellises, and other upright supports.

More ground covers can be found among the encyclopedia entries for herbs, annuals, perennials, and ornamental grasses.

Trumpet creeper

(*Campsis radicans*)

WATER USE: Low to moderate, tolerates drought, adaptable

HARDINESS: Zones 4 to 9

SITE: Sun and most soils

CHARACTERISTICS: This easy-growing vine can reach 40 feet long and uses clinging roots to climb trees, fences, and trellises. It has handsome compound leaves over a foot long. Through much of summer it flaunts red or orange trumpet-shaped flowers that attract hummingbirds.

LANDSCAPE USE: Screen, trellis, fence

Winter creeper

(*Euonymus fortunei*)

WATER USE: Moderate, tolerates short periods of drought

HARDINESS: Zones 5 to 9

SITE: Sun to partial shade and well-drained soil

CHARACTERISTICS: This evergreen has glossy green foliage sometimes brightened with gold or white variegation. As a ground cover, it may creep along the earth, reaching only 6 inches high and spreading from about 18 inches to many feet wide, depending on the cultivar. It will also climb, shimmying as high as 50 feet up a tree trunk. Some cultivars are compact shrubs that stay in tidy mounds.

LANDSCAPE USE: Ground cover, evergreen vine, shrub border

Creeping juniper

(*Juniperus horizontalis*)

WATER USE: Moderate, tolerates drought, adaptable

HARDINESS: Zones 3 to 9

SITE: Sun and well-drained to moderately moist soil

CHARACTERISTICS: This popular low-growing evergreen has attractive sprays of blue- or gray-green foliage that change to purple in winter. It may reach 2 feet high, with a spread of up to 10 feet, but size varies greatly with the cultivar.

LANDSCAPE USE: Foundation, shrub border, ground cover, container, bank

Kamschatka sedum

(*Sedum kamtschaticum*)

WATER USE: Low to moderate, tolerates drought

HARDINESS: Zones 3 to 8

SITE: Sun or light shade and well-drained soil

CHARACTERISTICS: This creeping perennial has fleshy, toothed leaves, which are attractively variegated in some cultivars. Clusters of yellow, star-shaped flowers appear in summer. *Kamschatka sedum* can reach to 12 inches tall.

LANDSCAPE USE: Perennial garden, ground cover

Mother-of-thyme

(*Thymus serpyllum*)

WATER USE: Low to moderate, tolerates drought

HARDINESS: Zones 4 to 8

SITE: Sun and well- to sharply drained soil

CHARACTERISTICS: This low shrub bears tiny, fragrant, and flavorful leaves that can be green, gray-green, or variegated with white or yellow, depending on the cultivar. While only 3 inches high, it may spread 3 feet wide. Small pink, red, or white flowers cover the plant in late spring or early summer.

LANDSCAPE USE: Ground cover, between rocks in walk or patio, rock garden, herb garden, slope

SHRUBS: Like perennials, many shrubs will tolerate dry soil or short droughts and are ideal for easy-care shrub borders or foundation plantings. However, they do need to be well established before being allowed to fend for themselves. In dry weather, soak young root systems deeply for a year or more after planting, until the shrubs are well rooted and growing strongly.

Lead plant

(*Amorpha canescens*)

WATER USE: Low, tolerates drought

HARDINESS: Zones 4 to 6

SITE: Sun and well-drained soil

CHARACTERISTICS: Furry, white shoots and fernlike, divided leaves set the stage for clusters of pea-shaped purple flowers that arrive late in summer and early in fall. Native to arid, sandy regions of North America, including the Great Plains, leguminous lead plant captures its own nitrogen with the help of nitrogen-fixing bacteria, and has a deep taproot. It can reach from 1 to 4 feet high and usually spreads to 4 feet wide.

LANDSCAPE USE: Dry bank, dry mixed border, shrub garden

Japanese barberry

(*Berberis thunbergii*)

WATER USE: Low to moderate

HARDINESS: Zones 4 to 8

SITE: Sun and well-drained soil

CHARACTERISTICS: One of the biggest attractions of this shrub are the small, oval leaves that clothe the plant in green, purple, and gold, depending on the cultivar. It grows into modest-sized mounds from 3 to 5 feet high. Most cultivars are thorny, with a few excep-

tions. Small, yellow spring flowers mature into attractive red berries for fall and winter interest.

LANDSCAPE USE: Foundation planting, mixed border, low hedge, barrier

Blue mist spirea or bluebeard

(*Caryopteris* × *clandonensis*)

WATER USE: Low to moderate

HARDINESS: Zones 5 to 9

SITE: Sun and well-drained soil

CHARACTERISTICS: Although usually pruned to the ground in winter and grown like a perennial, bluebeard is actually a shrub. It reaches 3 feet high and bears attractive gray-green leaves. Abundant clusters of blue or purple flowers cover new wood in late summer.

LANDSCAPE USE: Shrub border, perennial garden, mixed border

Smoke tree

(*Cotinus coggygria*)

WATER USE: Moderate, adaptable

HARDINESS: Zones 5 to 8 or 9

SITE: Sun and well-drained soil

CHARACTERISTICS: This tall shrub, which can grow 15 feet high, is famous for its late spring or early summer flowers. The yellow flowers are tiny but bear long hairs of pink or purple, which look like smoke. The oval leaves may be green or purple, depending on the cultivar.

LANDSCAPE USE: Shrub border, masses, mixed border

Cranberry cotoneaster
(Cotoneaster apiculatus)

WATER USE: Moderate, tolerates drought

HARDINESS: Zones 4 to 7

SITE: Sun and moist, well-drained soil

CHARACTERISTICS: Reaching 3 feet high and up to 6 feet wide, this shrub has intriguing herringbone branching and petite shiny green leaves. It can be covered with small pink flowers in spring, which are followed by red berries.

LANDSCAPE USE: Foundation planting, shrub border, mixed border, bank, edging retaining wall

Spreading cotoneaster
(Cotoneaster divaricatus)

WATER USE: Moderate, tolerates low water

HARDINESS: Zones 5 to 8

SITE: Sun and moist, well-drained soil

CHARACTERISTICS: While it can reach 5 feet tall, the spreading cotoneaster usually stays smaller and has a wider spread. It bears white or pink flowers in late spring, red berries in summer and fall, and small, shiny, oval leaves that turn red in autumn.

LANDSCAPE USE: Hedge, screen, bank planting, cascading edging for retaining wall, wildlife garden

Rockspray cotoneaster
(Cotoneaster horizontalis)

WATER USE: Moderate, tolerates low water

HARDINESS: Zones 4 to 7

SITE: Sun and moist, well-drained soil

CHARACTERISTICS: This cotoneaster is similar to the spreading cotoneaster except it reaches 3 feet high and can spread 8 feet wide, creating bold horizontal lines in the landscape. The flowers are pink and the berries are red.

LANDSCAPE USE: Ground cover, bank, shrub bed, mixed border

Russian olive
(Elaeagnus angustifolia)

WATER USE: Low to moderate, adaptable

HARDINESS: Zones 2 to 7

SITE: Sun, most soils

CHARACTERISTICS: Here is an adaptable Eurasian plant that has escaped in America and can be seen growing wild along many roadsides. It is easily identified by its long silver leaves and open thorny branches. It grows 12 to 20 feet high, bearing fragrant yellow flowers in spring followed by sweet yellow berries in fall. The berries may be eaten by birds and spread far and wide in their droppings, giving this shrub the reputation of a weed.

LANDSCAPE USE: Hedge, wildlife garden, naturalizing, shrub border

Sea buckthorn
(Hippophae rhamnoides)

WATER USE: Low to moderate, tolerates drought, adaptable

HARDINESS: Zones 3 to 8

SITE: Sun and well-drained, preferably infertile, soil

CHARACTERISTICS: A Eurasian native of dry dunes and rocky mountainsides, this shrub has narrow, silvery leaves. Its small spring flowers mature to orange fruit on female plants in late summer. Both male and female sea buckthorns can reach to 20 feet high and spread with suckering stems to 20 feet wide.

LANDSCAPE USE: Bank, informal hedge, barrier, wildlife garden

Aaron's beard Saint-John's-wort

(*Hypericum calycinum*)

WATER USE: Low to moderate

HARDINESS: Zones 5 to 8

SITE: Sun and well-drained to poor sandy soils

CHARACTERISTICS: This creeping semi-evergreen shrub is related to *Hypericum perforatum* from which the herbal antidepressant Saint John's-wort is extracted. It reaches about 18 inches high and often spreads slightly wider. It has narrow green leaves and bright displays of open-faced yellow flowers in summer.

LANDSCAPE USE: Shrub border, mixed border, rock garden

Rocky Mountain juniper

(*Juniperus scopulorum*)

WATER USE: Low to moderate, tolerates drought, adaptable

HARDINESS: Zones 3 to 7

SITE: Sun and well-drained soil

CHARACTERISTICS: Almost as if it had multiple personalities, this upright shrub or conical tree can reach 30 feet high but is also available in cultivars that stay as low as 2 to 4 feet high. The foliage is green, blue-green, or silvery, with scalelike leaves set in plumed branchlets. Dark blue berries attract birds.

LANDSCAPE USE: Shrub border, screen, hedge, specimen, wildlife garden

Beauty bush

(*Kolkwitzia amabilis*)

WATER USE: Moderate, tolerates some drought

HARDINESS: Zones 4 to 8

SITE: Sun to light shade and well-drained soil

CHARACTERISTICS: This 6- to 10-foot-tall shrub achieves its peak of beauty in late spring and early summer when covered with pink flowers. The flowers are followed by brown capsules. The leaves are oval.

LANDSCAPE USE: Specimen, shrub border

Bush cinquefoil

(*Potentilla fruticosa*)

WATER USE: Moderate, tolerates some drought

HARDINESS: Zones 2 to 7

SITE: Sun to light shade and fertile, well-drained soil

CHARACTERISTICS: This modest-sized shrub is anything but modest when it comes to flowers. Beginning in summer and continuing sporadically into fall, it bears open-faced flowers of yellow, white, cream, orange, pink, or red, depending on the cultivar. The leaves are finely textured. The shrubs grow from 1 to 4 feet high with a similar width, a range that also varies with the cultivar.

LANDSCAPE USE: Shrub border, foundation planting, mixed border, informal hedge, clusters and masses

Staghorn sumac

(*Rhus typhina*)

WATER USE: Low to moderate, tolerates drought, adaptable

HARDINESS: Zones 3 to 8

SITE: Sun to partial shade and well-drained soil

CHARACTERISTICS: A native American plant common along roadsides and meadows through much of the eastern United States, staghorn sumac grows in colonies 10 to 25 feet high. It has elongated compound leaves, which turn stunning shades of orange, red, or yellow in fall. The shrub has an open form, graceful branching, and long-lasting clusters of woolly red fruit; however, it can be an aggressive spreader.

LANDSCAPE USE: Masses, bank, large native garden

Rugosa rose

(*Rosa rugosa*)

WATER USE: Moderate, tolerates some drought

HARDINESS: Zones 3 to 7

SITE: Full sun and organic, rich, well-drained soil

CHARACTERISTICS: One of the easiest roses to grow, a rugosa rose can thrive even in salty seashore sites. It grows 4 to 6 feet high, depending on the cultivar, and bears large, single or double blossoms from early summer into fall. The

flowers may be pink, red, rose, lilac, or white; some are fragrant. In late summer and fall, they are followed by red rose hips. The leaves are disease resistant and the stems are clad with thorns.

LANDSCAPE USE: Hedge, shrub border, mixed border, rose garden

Vanhoutte spirea

(*Spiraea* × *Vanhouttei*)

WATER USE: Moderate, adaptable

HARDINESS: Zones 3 to 8

SITE: Sun to light shade and most soils

CHARACTERISTICS: This old-fashioned shrub can grow for decades in a single site regardless of the changes in weather, making it a stalwart choice for a moderately moist garden. It bears sprays of white flowers in late spring or early summer, has toothed oval leaves, and upright arching stems reaching to about 8 feet high

LANDSCAPE USE: Specimen, informal hedge, mixed border

Lilac

(*Syringa vulgaris*)

WATER USE: Moderate to moist, tolerates some drought

HARDINESS: Zones 3 to 7

SITE: Sun and moist, well-drained soil

CHARACTERISTICS: A durable and long-lived shrub, the lilac is famous for its fragrant spring clusters of flowers that can be purple, white, blue, lilac, or pink, depending on the cultivar. It can grow from 8 to 25 feet high and has heart-shaped leaves easily attacked by powdery mildew.

LANDSCAPE USE: Shrub border, groups, mixed border, pruned into small tree

Wayfaring tree

(*Viburnum lantana*)

WATER USE: Moderate

HARDINESS: Zones 4 to 8

SITE: Sun to partial shade and moist, well-drained soil

CHARACTERISTICS: This viburnum has handsome clusters of white spring flowers followed by bird-attracting berries that change from yellow to red and black. A big, bold plant, it reaches 10 to 15 feet high with similar spread. The oval leaves are touched with gray below.

LANDSCAPE USE: Informal hedge, screen, mixed border, specimen, cluster, wildlife garden

TREES: Because trees will be a long-term investment for your yard, choose a species that will thrive with the natural rainfall of the region. Young trees can and should be watered until well established, but mature trees with a large root spread will be much more difficult to irrigate thoroughly. It is better to start with species that can be self-sufficient.

Amur maple

(*Acer ginnala* syn. *A. tataricum* subsp. *ginnala*)

WATER USE: Low to moderate, somewhat adaptable

HARDINESS: Zones 2 to 8

SITE: Sun to light shade and moist, well-drained soil

CHARACTERISTICS: This small, often multistemmed maple reaches 15 to 20 feet high, with a spread up to 25 feet wide. The leaves are three- to five-lobed and turn red in fall. The small spring flowers are followed by flat, winged, red fruit that can brighten the tree into late fall.

LANDSCAPE USE: Specimen, screen, shade in small spaces, patio tree

Hedge maple

(*Acer campestre*)

WATER USE: Moderate, adaptable

HARDINESS: Zones 4 or 5 to 8

SITE: Sun to light shade and rich, well-drained soil

CHARACTERISTICS: Another small maple, this tree reaches 25 to 35 feet tall and usually has multiple trunks that make a row of hedge maples ideal for clipping into a large hedge. The lobed leaves turn yellow in fall.

LANDSCAPE USE: Small lawn tree, street tree, hedge

Northern catalpa

(*Catalpa speciosa*)

WATER USE: Low to moderate to moist, adaptable

HARDINESS: Zones 4 to 8

SITE: Sun and deep, rich soil

CHARACTERISTICS: This easy-growing tree tolerates many conditions but usually needs irrigation during drought. It is a flashy tree with heart-shaped leaves and big clusters of fragrant white flowers in early summer. They are followed by legumelike pods that reach 15 inches long. Although interesting to look at, the pods can make a mess if the tree is planted over a driveway or patio. Northern catalpas reach 40 to 70 feet high.

LANDSCAPE USE: Specimen tree, shade tree

Hackberry

(*Celtis occidentalis*)

WATER USE: Low to moderate to moist, adaptable

HARDINESS: Zones 4 to 9

SITE: Sun to light shade and rich, moist soil

CHARACTERISTICS: This native American tree is a familiar sight along rivers, in fields, or by dry roadsides. It is ultimately adaptable, which makes it a great candidate for a water-conserving garden. The tree reaches 50 to 60 feet high and has an oval canopy. It has toothed leaves and a berry that turns from red to purple in autumn. A major downfall is its susceptibility to attack by many insects and disease.

LANDSCAPE USE: Street tree, shade, windbreak

Turkish filbert

(*Corylus colurna*)

WATER USE: Moderate, tolerates some drought

HARDINESS: Zones 5 to 7

SITE: Sun and rich, well-drained soil

CHARACTERISTICS: This tree, which reaches 40 to 70 feet tall, produces edible nuts and makes an attractive specimen tree. It forms an upright, pyramidal shape and has oval toothed leaves. Dangling yellow flowers, called catkins, emerge in late winter or early spring. Female flowers bear clusters of nuts in late summer and fall.

LANDSCAPE USE: Lawn tree, edible ornamental garden

Cockspur hawthorn

(*Crataegus crus-galli*)

WATER USE: Moderate

HARDINESS: Zones 3 to 7

SITE: Sun and well-drained soil

CHARACTERISTICS: Reaching 20 to 30 feet high, this small ornamental tree has attractive horizontal branching. In spring, it bears clusters of white flowers followed by red berries. The leaves turn red in fall. While the species has long thorns, the variety *inermis* is thornless and safe to grow around playgrounds.

LANDSCAPE USE: Specimen, grouping, screen, hedge, barrier

Hardy rubber tree

(*Eucommia ulmoides*)

WATER USE: Moderate, tolerates drought, adaptable

HARDINESS: Zones 4 to 7

SITE: Sun and well-drained soil

CHARACTERISTICS: A small amount of rubber is contained in the sap of this uncommon shade tree. The leaves are toothed and elliptic. The tree grows 40 to 60 feet high with similar spread.

LANDSCAPE USE: Shade tree

Green ash

(*Fraxinus pennsylvanica*)

WATER USE: Low, moderate, or moist,

tolerates drought, adaptable

HARDINESS: Zones 4 to 9

SITE: Sun and most soils

CHARACTERISTICS: This well-rounded tree can grow easily in many locations. It reaches 50 to 60 feet high and 25 to 30 feet wide. The compound leaves change to yellow in fall. The winged fruit, which are abundant on female trees, can sprout everywhere. Avoid self-sowing by purchasing seedless cultivars. The root system is shallow but wide spreading.

LANDSCAPE USE: Specimen, screen, shade, windbreak, street tree

Thornless honey locust

(*Gleditsia triacanthos* var. *inermis*)

WATER USE: Moderate, tolerates drought

HARDINESS: Zones 3 to 9

SITE: Sun and well-drained to rich, moist soil

CHARACTERISTICS: Although prone to problems with insects and diseases and accused of being overused, the honey locust grows well in many locations. It reaches 30 to 70 feet high, depending on the cultivar. The feathery, compound leaves, which reach 8 inches long, turn yellow in fall. Clusters of small but fragrant whitish flowers appear in spring and mature to interesting twisted, brown, legumelike seed pods to 18 inches long.

LANDSCAPE USE: Shade tree, patio tree

Kentucky coffee tree

(*Gymnocladus dioica*)

WATER USE: Moderate to moist, tolerates some drought, adaptable

HARDINESS: Zones 3 to 8

SITE: Sun and rich, well-drained soil

CHARACTERISTICS: While most trees mix their male and female flowers, Kentucky coffee trees are limited to either one or the other. Female trees have large panicles of fragrant whitish flowers in spring that mature into long pods of dark seeds that look a little like coffee beans but are poisonous. Male trees have shorter flower clusters and no pods. The leaves are feathery and compound, reaching to 24 inches long and turning gold in fall. The tree can reach 50 to 60 feet tall and has a rounded shape.

LANDSCAPE USE: Shade tree, specimen, or street tree

Golden rain tree

(*Koelreuteria paniculata*)

WATER USE: Moderate, tolerates water and drought, adaptable

HARDINESS: Zones 5 to 9

SITE: Sun and most soils

CHARACTERISTICS: This moderate-sized tree reaches 20 to 30 feet tall and bears 15-inch-long clusters of yellow flowers in midsummer. They are followed by papery seed pods that change from green to tan and can last the winter. The feathery compound leaves reach 14 inches long and turn yellow in fall.

LANDSCAPE USE: Accent, specimen, shade tree for small spaces

Austrian pine

(*Pinus nigra*)

WATER USE: Moderate to moist, tolerates some drought, adaptable

HARDINESS: Zones 4 to 7

SITE: Sun and moist soils

CHARACTERISTICS: This durable pine, which has a narrow, upright shape, reaches 50 to 60 feet high. The stiff dark green needles are borne in bunches of two. The pine cones are oval. Unfortunately, Austrian pines in some regions may die back due to a blight disease and other complications.

LANDSCAPE USE: Screen, specimen, windbreak

Ponderosa pine

(*Pinus ponderosa*)

WATER USE: Moderate, tolerates drought

HARDINESS: Zones 3 to 7

SITE: Sun and deep, moist, well-drained soil

CHARACTERISTICS: The deep taproot can support this western United States native during short droughts. It grows into a narrow pyramid, reaching 80 to 100 feet tall. The needles are held in bunches of two or three and the cones are egg-shaped.

LANDSCAPE USE: Specimen, focal point, masses

Japanese black pine

(*Pinus thunbergiana*)

WATER USE: Low to moderate, tolerates drought, adaptable

HARDINESS: Zones 5 to 8

SITE: Sun and moist, fertile, well-drained soil

CHARACTERISTICS: Intriguing twisted needles are one characteristic of the Japanese black pine. It grows into an open pyramid 20 to 70 feet high, depending on the cultivar. Dwarf forms are available that stay only a couple of

feet high and can be used like shrubs.

LANDSCAPE USE: Screen, informal garden, stablizer for sand dunes, accent

Chinese pistache

(*Pistacia chinensis*)

WATER USE: Moderate, adaptable, tolerates drought

HARDINESS: Zones 6 to 9

SITE: Sun and moist, well-drained soil

CHARACTERISTICS: A moderate-sized tree, Chinese pistache reaches 30 to 35 feet high. It has 10-inch-long compound leaves that change to orange or red in autumn. Small spring flowers turn into bird-attracting blue or red berries in fall

LANDSCAPE USE: Shade tree, street tree, wildlife garden

Swamp white oak

(*Quercus bicolor*)

WATER USE: Low to moderate to moist, tolerates drought, adaptable

HARDINESS: Zones 3 to 8

SITE: Sun to light shade and acidic soil

CHARACTERISTICS: This popular native tree is found in swampy areas but is also able to tolerate drought. It grows 40 to 50 feet high and has acorns and round-lobed leaves that change to yellow or purple-red in fall.

LANDSCAPE USE: Shade tree

Bur oak

(*Quercus macrocarpa*)

WATER USE: Low to moderate to moist, adaptable

HARDINESS: Zones 2 to 8

SITE: Sun and many soils

CHARACTERISTICS: Another versatile tree, the bur oak can grow 60 to 80 feet high and has a spreading crown. The deeply lobed leaves turn yellowish brown in fall. The acorn can be fringed, which explains another common name for it—mossy-cup oak.

LANDSCAPE USE: Shade tree

New Mexico locust

(Robinia neomexicana)

WATER USE: Low to moderate, tolerates drought, adaptable

HARDINESS: Zones 5 to 9

SITE: Sun and well-drained soil

CHARACTERISTICS: This small, spiny tree, which also can sucker into a shrub form, is native to the arid North American Southwest. It has flamboyant, dangling clusters of pink flowers in early summer that mature to dark pods. The leaves, like those of other locusts, are pinnately divided like a feather. It can grow to 20 feet high and spread like a shrub to 15 feet wide. Like the lead plant, new Mexico locust is a legume that can capture its own nitrogen.

LANDSCAPE USE: Dry bank, informal hedge, ornamental tree

Japanese pagoda tree

(Sophora japonica)

WATER USE: Moderate, tolerates drought

HARDINESS: Zones 4 to 8

SITE: Sun and well-drained soil

CHARACTERISTICS: This tree, which grows 40 to 75 feet high, has clusters of white bell-shaped flowers in late summer and elongated pods in fall and winter. The compound leaves reach 9 inches long. Weeping and narrow, upright columnar forms are available.

LANDSCAPE USE: Specimen, shade tree, street tree

Japanese zelkova

(Zelkova serrata)

WATER USE: Moderate to moist, tolerates drought

HARDINESS: Zones 5 to 8

SITE: Sun and deep, moist soil

CHARACTERISTICS: Looking much like an elm, this tree grows 50 to 80 feet high and has oval toothed leaves that turn yellow-brown or red in fall.

LANDSCAPE USE: Shade tree

INDEX

(Page numbers in italics refer to illustrations.)